Contents

SEVEN LAYER TACO DIP
Servings: 56 | Prep: 30m | Cooks: 0m | Total: 30m

NUTRITION FACTS

Calories: 66 | Carbohydrates: 3.5g | Fat: 4.9g | Protein: 2.3g | Cholesterol: 13mg

INGREDIENTS

- 1 (1 ounce) package taco seasoning mix
- 1 green bell pepper, chopped
- 1 (16 ounce) can refried beans
- 1 bunch chopped green onions
- 1 (8 ounce) package cream cheese, softened
- 1 small head iceberg lettuce, shredded
- 1 (16 ounce) container sour cream
- 1 (6 ounce) can sliced black olives, drained
- 1 (16 ounce) jar salsa
- 2 cups shredded Cheddar cheese
- 1 large tomato, chopped

DIRECTIONS

1. Combine rice and water in a medium saucepan. Bring to a boil over high heat. Reduce heat to low, cover with lid, and allow to steam until tender, about 20 minutes.
2. While rice is cooking, grind peanuts in a blender and set aside. Heat the margarine in a skillet over medium heat. Stir in the onion; cook and stir until the onion has softened and turned golden brown about 10 minutes. Stir in ginger, carrots, and salt to taste. Reduce heat to low and cover to steam 5 minutes. Stir in cayenne pepper and peanuts. When rice is done, add it to skillet and stir gently to combine with other ingredients. Garnish with chopped cilantro.

ADDICTIVE SWEET POTATO BURRITOS
Servings: 12 | Prep: 15m | Cooks: 25m | Total: 40m

NUTRITION FACTS

Calories: 505 | Carbohydrates: 76.6g | Fat: 8.5g | Protein: 20g | Cholesterol: 20mg

INGREDIENTS

- 1 tablespoon vegetable oil
- 2 teaspoons ground cumin
- 1 onion, chopped
- 1 pinch cayenne pepper, or to taste

- 4 cloves garlic, minced
- 3 tablespoons soy sauce
- 6 cups canned kidney beans, drained
- 4 cups mashed cooked sweet potatoes
- 2 cups water
- 12 (10 inch) flour tortillas, warmed
- 3 tablespoons chili powder
- 8 ounces shredded Cheddar cheese
- 4 teaspoons prepared mustard

DIRECTIONS

1. Preheat oven to 350 degrees F (175 degrees C).
2. Heat oil in a medium skillet and saute onion and garlic until soft. Mash beans into the onion mixture. Gradually stir in water; heat until warm, 2 to 3 minutes. Remove from heat and stir in the soy sauce, chili powder, mustard, cumin, and cayenne pepper.
3. Divide bean mixture and mashed sweet potatoes evenly between the tortillas; top with cheese. Fold tortillas burrito-style around the fillings and place on a baking sheet.
4. Bake in the preheated oven until warmed through, about 12 minutes.

FISH TACOS

Servings: 8 | Prep: 40m | Cooks: 20m | Total: 1h

NUTRITION FACTS

Calories: 409 | Carbohydrates: 43g | Fat: 18.8g | Protein: 17.3g | Cholesterol: 54mg

INGREDIENTS

- 1 cup all-purpose flour
- 1 teaspoon minced capers
- 2 tablespoons cornstarch
- 1/2 teaspoon dried oregano
- 1 teaspoon baking powder
- 1/2 teaspoon ground cumin
- 1/2 teaspoon salt
- 1/2 teaspoon dried dill weed
- 1 egg
- 1 teaspoon ground cayenne pepper
- 1 cup beer
- 1 quart oil for frying
- 1/2 cup plain yogurt
- 1 pound cod fillets, cut into 2 to 3 ounce portions

- 1/2 cup mayonnaise
- 1 (12 ounce) package corn tortillas
- 1 lime, juiced
- 1/2 medium head cabbage, finely shredded
- 1 jalapeno pepper, minced

DIRECTIONS

1. To make beer batter: In a large bowl, combine flour, cornstarch, baking powder, and salt. Blend egg and beer, then quickly stir into the flour mixture (don't worry about a few lumps).
2. To make white sauce: In a medium bowl, mix together yogurt and mayonnaise. Gradually stir in fresh lime juice until consistency is slightly runny. Season with jalapeno, capers, oregano, cumin, dill, and cayenne.
3. Heat oil in deep-fryer to 375 degrees F (190 degrees C).
4. Dust fish pieces lightly with flour. Dip into beer batter, and fry until crisp and golden brown. Drain on paper towels. Lightly fry tortillas; not too crisp. To serve, place fried fish in a tortilla, and top with shredded cabbage, and white sauce.

MEXICAN BEAN SALAD

Servings: 8 | Prep: 15m | Cooks: 0m | Total: 1h15m

NUTRITION FACTS

Calories: 334 | Carbohydrates: 41.7g | Fat: 14.8g | Protein: 11.2g | Cholesterol: 0mg

INGREDIENTS

- 1 (15 ounce) can black beans, rinsed and drained
- 1 tablespoon lemon juice
- 1 (15 ounce) can kidney beans, drained
- 2 tablespoons white sugar
- 1 (15 ounce) can cannellini beans, drained and rinsed
- 1 tablespoon salt
- 1 green bell pepper, chopped
- 1 clove crushed garlic
- 1 red bell pepper, chopped
- 1/4 cup chopped fresh cilantro
- 1 (10 ounce) package frozen corn kernels
- 1/2 tablespoon ground cumin
- 1 red onion, chopped
- 1/2 tablespoon ground black pepper
- 1/2 cup olive oil
- 1 dash hot pepper sauce
- 1/2 cup red wine vinegar

- 1/2 teaspoon chili powder
- 2 tablespoons fresh lime juice

DIRECTIONS

1. In a large bowl, combine beans, bell peppers, frozen corn, and red onion.
2. In a small bowl, whisk together olive oil, red wine vinegar, lime juice, lemon juice, sugar, salt, garlic, cilantro, cumin, and black pepper. Season to taste with hot sauce and chili powder.
3. Pour olive oil dressing over vegetables; mix well. Chill thoroughly, and serve cold.

LIME CHICKEN SOFT TACOS
Servings: 10 | Prep: 20m | Cooks: 30m | Total: 50m

NUTRITION FACTS

Calories: 204 | Carbohydrates: 18.9g | Fat: 6.8g | Protein: 16.2g | Cholesterol: 37mg

INGREDIENTS

- 1 1/2 pounds skinless, boneless chicken breast meat - cubed
- 2 cloves garlic, minced
- 1/8 cup red wine vinegar
- 1 teaspoon dried oregano
- 1/2 lime, juiced
- 10 (6 inch) flour tortillas
- 1 teaspoon white sugar
- 1 tomato, diced
- 1/2 teaspoon salt
- 1/4 cup shredded lettuce
- 1/2 teaspoon ground black pepper
- 1/4 cup shredded Monterey Jack cheese
- 2 green onions, chopped
- 1/4 cup salsa

DIRECTIONS

1. Saute chicken in a medium saucepan over medium high heat for about 20 minutes. Add vinegar, lime juice, sugar, salt, pepper, green onion, garlic and oregano. Simmer for an extra 10 minutes.
2. Heat an iron skillet over medium heat. Place a tortilla in the pan, warm, and turn over to heat the other side. Repeat with remaining tortillas. Serve lime chicken mixture in warm tortillas topped with tomato, lettuce, cheese and salsa.

SOPAPILLA CHEESECAKE PIE
Servings: 12 | Prep: 15m | Cooks: 45m | Total: 3h | Additional: 2h

NUTRITION FACTS

Calories: 481 | Carbohydrates: 50.8g | Fat: 28.7g | Protein: 5.6g | Cholesterol: 61mg

INGREDIENTS

- 2 (8 ounce) packages cream cheese, softened
- 1 teaspoon ground cinnamon
- 13/4 cups white sugar, divided
- 1/2 cup butter, room temperature
- 1 teaspoon Mexican vanilla extract
- 1/4 cup honey
- 2 (8 ounce) cans refrigerated crescent rolls

DIRECTIONS

1. Preheat an oven to 350 degrees F (175 degrees C). Prepare a 9x13 inch baking dish with cooking spray.
2. Beat the cream cheese with 1 cup of sugar and the vanilla extract in a bowl until smooth.
3. Unroll the cans of crescent roll dough, and use a rolling pin to shape each piece into 9x13 inch rectangles. Press one piece into the bottom of a 9x13 inch baking dish. Evenly spread the cream cheese mixture into the baking dish, then cover with the remaining piece of crescent dough. Stir together 3/4 cup of sugar, cinnamon, and butter. Dot the mixture over the top of the cheesecake.
4. Bake in the preheated oven until the crescent dough has puffed and turned golden brown, about 30 minutes. Remove from the oven and drizzle with honey. Cool completely in the pan before cutting into 12 squares.

REFRIED BEANS WITHOUT THE REFRY
Servings: 15 | Prep: 15m | Cooks: 8h | Total: 8h15m

NUTRITION FACTS

Calories: 139 | Carbohydrates: 25.4g | Fat: 0.5g | Protein: 8.5g | Cholesterol: 0mg

INGREDIENTS

- 1 onion, peeled and halved
- 5 teaspoons salt
- 3 cups dry pinto beans, rinsed
- 1 3/4 teaspoons fresh ground black pepper
- 1/2 fresh jalapeno pepper, seeded and chopped

- 1/8 teaspoon ground cumin, optional
- 2 tablespoons minced garlic
- 9 cups water

DIRECTIONS

1. Place the onion, rinsed beans, jalapeno, garlic, salt, pepper, and cumin into a slow cooker. Pour in the water and stir to combine. Cook on High for 8 hours, adding more water as needed. Note: if more than 1 cup of water has evaporated during cooking, then the temperature is too high.
2. Once the beans have cooked, strain them, and reserve the liquid. Mash the beans with a potato masher, adding the reserved water as needed to attain desired consistency.

EASY MEXICAN CASSEROLE
Servings: 6 | Prep: 20m | Cooks: 30m | Total: 50m

NUTRITION FACTS

Calories: 632 | Carbohydrates: 32.8g | Fat: 43.7g | Protein: 31.7g | Cholesterol: 119mg

INGREDIENTS

- 1 pound lean ground beef
- 1 (2 ounce) can sliced black olives, drained
- 2 cups salsa
- 1/2 cup chopped green onion
- 1 (16 ounce) can chili beans, drained
- 1/2 cup chopped fresh tomato
- 3 cups tortilla chips, crushed
- 2 cups shredded Cheddar chees
- 2 cups sour cream

DIRECTIONS

1. Preheat oven to 350 degrees F (175 degrees C).
2. In a large skillet over medium-high heat, cook ground beef until no longer pink. Stir in salsa, reduce heat, and simmer 20 minutes, or until liquid is absorbed. Stir in beans, and heat through.
3. Spray a 9x13 baking dish with cooking spray. Spread crushed tortilla chips in dish, and then spoon beef mixture over chips. Spread sour cream over beef, and sprinkle olives, green onion, and tomato over the sour cream. Top with Cheddar cheese.
4. Bake in preheated oven for 30 minutes, or until hot and bubbly.

CATHERINE'S SPICY CHICKEN SOUP
Servings: 8 | Prep: 15m | Cooks: 30m | Total: 45m

NUTRITION FACTS

Calories: 473 | Carbohydrates: 50.3g | Fat: 15.3g | Protein: 36.9g | Cholesterol: 82mg

INGREDIENTS

- 2 quarts water
- 3 cloves garlic, chopped
- 8 skinless, boneless chicken breast halves
- 1 (16 ounce) jar chunky salsa
- 1/2 teaspoon salt
- 2 (14.5 ounce) cans peeled and diced tomatoes
- 1 teaspoon ground black pepper
- 1 (14.5 ounce) can whole peeled tomatoes
- 1 teaspoon garlic powder
- 1 (10.75 ounce) can condensed tomato soup
- 2 tablespoons dried parsley
- 3 tablespoons chili powder
- 1 tablespoon onion powder
- 1 (15 ounce) can whole kernel corn, drained
- 5 cubes chicken bouillon
- 2 (16 ounce) cans chili beans, undrained
- 3 tablespoons olive oil
- 1 (8 ounce) container sour cream
- 1 onion, chopped

DIRECTIONS

1. In a large pot over medium heat, combine water, chicken, salt, pepper, garlic powder, parsley, onion powder and bouillon cubes. Bring to a boil, then reduce heat and simmer 1 hour, or until chicken juices run clear. Remove chicken, reserve broth. Shred chicken.
2. In a large pot over medium heat, cook onion and garlic in olive oil until slightly browned. Stir in salsa, diced tomatoes, whole tomatoes, tomato soup, chili powder, corn, chili beans, sour cream, shredded chicken and 5 cups broth. Simmer 30 minutes.

SLOW COOKER TACO SOUP
Servings: 8 | Prep: 10m | Cooks: 8h | Total: 8h10m

NUTRITION FACTS

Calories: 362 | Carbohydrates: 37.8g | Fat: 16.3g | Protein: 18.2g | Cholesterol: 48mg

INGREDIENTS

- 1 pound ground beef
- 1 (8 ounce) can tomato sauce
- 1 onion, chopped
- 2 cups water
- 1 (16 ounce) can chili beans, with liquid
- 2 (14.5 ounce) cans peeled and diced tomatoes
- 1 (15 ounce) can kidney beans with liquid
- 1 (4 ounce) can diced green chile peppers
- 1 (15 ounce) can whole kernel corn, with liquid
- 1 (1.25 ounce) package taco seasoning mix

DIRECTIONS

1. In a medium skillet, cook the ground beef until browned over medium heat. Drain, and set aside.
2. Place the ground beef, onion, chili beans, kidney beans, corn, tomato sauce, water, diced tomatoes, green chile peppers and taco seasoning mix in a slow cooker. Mix to blend, and cook on Low setting for 8 hours.

DELICIOUS BLACK BEAN BURRITOS

Servings: 8 | Prep: 10m | Cooks: 15m | Total: 25m

NUTRITION FACTS

Calories: 692 | Carbohydrates: 70.2g | Fat: 35.8g | Protein: 21.2g | Cholesterol: 47mg

INGREDIENTS

- 2 (10 inch) flour tortillas
- 1 (15 ounce) can black beans, rinsed and drained
- 2 tablespoons vegetable oil
- 1 teaspoon minced jalapeno peppers
- 1 small onion, chopped
- 3 ounces cream cheese
- 1/2 red bell pepper, chopped
- 1/2 teaspoon salt
- 1 teaspoon minced garlic
- 2 tablespoons chopped fresh cilantro

DIRECTIONS

1. Wrap tortillas in foil and place in oven heated to 350 degrees F (175 degrees C). Bake for 15 minutes or until heated through.
2. Heat oil in a 10-inch skillet over medium heat. Place onion, bell pepper, garlic and jalapenos in skillet, cook for 2 minutes stirring occasionally. Pour beans into skillet, cook 3 minutes stirring.

3. Cut cream cheese into cubes and add to skillet with salt. Cook for 2 minutes stirring occasionally. Stir cilantro into mixture.
4. Spoon mixture evenly down center of warmed tortilla and roll tortillas up. Serve immediately.

BLACK BEAN AND SALSA SOUP
Servings: 4 | Prep: 10m | Cooks: 10m | Total: 20m

NUTRITION FACTS

Calories: 240 | Carbohydrates: 34.5g | Fat: 5g | Protein: 13.3g | Cholesterol: 6mg

INGREDIENTS

- 2 (15 ounce) cans black beans, drained and rinsed
- 1 teaspoon ground cumin
- 1 1/2 cups vegetable broth
- 4 tablespoons sour cream
- 1 cup chunky salsa
- 2 tablespoons thinly sliced green onion

DIRECTIONS

1. In an electric food processor or blender, combine beans, broth, salsa, and cumin. Blend until fairly smooth.
2. Heat the bean mixture in a saucepan over medium heat until thoroughly heated.
3. Ladle soup into 4 individual bowls, and top each bowl with 1 tablespoon of the sour cream and 1/2 tablespoon green onion.

SLOW COOKER CARNITAS
Servings: 10 | Prep: 10m | Cooks: 10m | Total: 10h10m

NUTRITION FACTS

Calories: 223 | Carbohydrates: 0.7g | Fat: 13.8g | Protein: 22.2g | Cholesterol: 73mg

INGREDIENTS

- 1 teaspoon salt
- 1/4 teaspoon ground cinnamon
- 1 teaspoon garlic powder
- 1 (4 pound) boneless pork shoulder roast
- 1 teaspoon ground cumin
- 2 bay leaves
- 1/2 teaspoon crumbled dried oregano

- 2 cups chicken broth
- 1/2 teaspoon ground coriander

DIRECTIONS

1. Mix together salt, garlic powder, cumin, oregano, coriander, and cinnamon in a bowl. Coat pork with the spice mixture. Place the bay leaves in the bottom of a slow cooker and place the pork on top. Pour the chicken broth around the sides of the pork, being careful not to rinse off the spice mixture.
2. Cover and cook on Low until the pork shreds easily with a fork, about 10 hours. Turn the meat after it has cooked for 5 hours. When the pork is tender, remove from slow cooker, and shred with two forks. Use cooking liquid as needed to moisten the meat.

BLACK BEAN AND CORN QUESADILLAS
Servings: 8 | Prep: 10m | Cooks: 30m | Total: 40m

NUTRITION FACTS

Calories: 363 | Carbohydrates: 45.6g | Fat: 14.5g | Protein: 13.9g | Cholesterol: 26mg

INGREDIENTS

- 2 teaspoons olive oil
- 1/4 cup salsa
- 3 tablespoons finely chopped onion
- 1/4 teaspoon red pepper flakes
- 1 (15.5 ounce) can black beans, drained and rinsed
- 2 tablespoons butter, divided
- 1 (10 ounce) can whole kernel corn, drained
- 8 (8 inch) flour tortillas
- 1 tablespoon brown sugar
- 1 1/2 cups shredded Monterey Jack cheese, divided

DIRECTIONS

1. Combine rice and water in a medium saucepan. Bring to a boil over high heat. Reduce heat to low, cover with lid, and allow to steam until tender, about 20 minutes.
2. While rice is cooking, grind peanuts in a blender and set aside. Heat the margarine in a skillet over medium heat. Stir in the onion; cook and stir until the onion has softened and turned golden brown about 10 minutes. Stir in ginger, carrots, and salt to taste. Reduce heat to low and cover to steam 5 minutes. Stir in cayenne pepper and peanuts. When rice is done, add it to skillet and stir gently to combine with other ingredients. Garnish with chopped cilantro.

CHICKEN TORTILLA SOUP

Servings: 8 | Prep: 20m | Cooks: 20m | Total: 40m

NUTRITION FACTS

Calories: 377 | Carbohydrates: 30.9g | Fat: 19.1g | Protein: 23.1g | Cholesterol: 46mg

INGREDIENTS

- 1 onion, chopped
- 1 cup white hominy
- 3 cloves garlic, minced
- 1 (4 ounce) can chopped green chile peppers
- 1 tablespoon olive oil
- 1 (15 ounce) can black beans, rinsed and drained
- 2 teaspoons chili powder
- ¼ cup chopped fresh cilantro
- 1 teaspoon dried oregano
- 2 boneless chicken breast halves, cooked and cut into bite-sized pieces
- 1 (28 ounce) can crushed tomatoes
- crushed tortilla chips
- 1 (10.5 ounce) can condensed chicken broth
- sliced avocado
- 1 ¼ cups water
- shredded Monterey Jack cheese
- 1 cup whole corn kernels, cooked
- chopped green onions

DIRECTIONS

1. In a medium stock pot, heat oil over medium heat. Saute onion and garlic in oil until soft. Stir in chili powder, oregano, tomatoes, broth, and water. Bring to a boil, and simmer for 5 to 10 minutes.
2. Stir in corn, hominy, chiles, beans, cilantro, and chicken. Simmer for 10 minutes.
3. Ladle soup into individual serving bowls, and top with crushed tortilla chips, avocado slices, cheese, and chopped green onion.

SPANISH RICE

Servings: 4 | Prep: 10m | Cooks: 30m | Total: 40m

NUTRITION FACTS

Calories: 270 | Carbohydrates: 45.7g | Fat: 7.6g | Protein: 4.8g | Cholesterol: 0mg

INGREDIENTS

- 2 tablespoons vegetable oil
- 2 cups water
- 1 cup uncooked white rice
- 1 (10 ounce) can diced tomatoes and green chiles
- 1 onion, chopped
- 2 teaspoons chili powder, or to taste
- 1/2 green bell pepper, chopped
- 1 teaspoon salt

DIRECTIONS

1. Heat oil in a deep skillet over medium heat. Saute rice, onion, and bell pepper until rice is browned and onions are tender.
2. Stir in water and tomatoes. Season with chili powder and salt. Cover, and simmer for 30 minutes, or until rice is cooked and liquid is absorbed.

SLOW COOKER CILANTRO LIME CHICKEN
Servings: 6 | Prep: 10m | Cooks: 4h | Total: 4h10m

NUTRITION FACTS

Calories: 272 | Carbohydrates: 9.3g | Fat: 4.7g | Protein: 45.3g | Cholesterol: 117mg

INGREDIENTS

- 1 (16 ounce) jar salsa
- 1 lime, juiced
- 1 (1.25 ounce) package dry taco seasoning mix
- 3 tablespoons chopped fresh cilantro
- 3 pounds skinless, boneless chicken breast halves

DIRECTIONS

1. Place the salsa, taco seasoning, lime juice, and cilantro into a slow cooker, and stir to combine. Add the chicken breasts, and stir to coat with the salsa mixture. Cover the cooker, set to High, and cook until the chicken is very tender, about 4 hours. If desired, set cooker to Low and cook 6 to 8 hours. Shred chicken with 2 forks to serve.

SALSA CHICKEN RICE CASSEROLE
Servings: 8 | Prep: 20m | Cooks: 1h | Total: 1h20m

NUTRITION FACTS

Calories: 477 | Carbohydrates: 34.8g | Fat: 23.9g | Protein: 30g | Cholesterol: 88mg

INGREDIENTS

- 1 1/3 cups uncooked white rice
- 1 (10.75 ounce) can condensed cream of chicken soup
- 2 2/3 cups water
- 1 (10.75 ounce) can condensed cream of mushroom soup
- 4 skinless, boneless chicken breast halves
- 1 onion, chopped
- 2 cups shredded Monterey Jack cheese
- 1 1/2 cups mild salsa
- 2 cups shredded Cheddar cheese

DIRECTIONS

1. Place rice and water in a saucepan, and bring to a boil. Reduce heat to low, cover, and simmer for 20 minutes.
2. Meanwhile, place chicken breast halves into a large saucepan, and fill the pan with water. Bring to a boil, and cook for 20 minutes, or until done. Remove chicken from water. When cool enough to handle, cut meat into bite-size pieces.
3. Preheat oven to 350 degrees F (175 degrees C). Lightly grease a 9x13 inch baking dish.
4. In a medium bowl, combine Monterey Jack and Cheddar cheeses. In a separate bowl, mix together cream of chicken soup, cream of mushroom soup, onion, and salsa. Layer 1/2 of the rice, 1/2 of the chicken, 1/2 of the soup and salsa mixture, and 1/2 of the cheese mixture in prepared dish. Repeat layers, ending with cheese.
5. Bake in preheated oven for about 40 minutes, or until bubbly.

MARINATED FLANK STEAK
Servings: 6 | Prep: 15m | Cooks: 10m | Total: 6h25m

NUTRITION FACTS

Calories: 275 | Carbohydrates: 3.4g | Fat: 22.5g | Protein: 14.8g | Cholesterol: 27mg

INGREDIENTS

- 1/2 cup vegetable oil
- 1 tablespoon Dijon mustard
- 1/3 cup soy sauce
- 2 cloves garlic, minced
- 1/4 cup red wine vinegar
- 1/2 teaspoon ground black pepper
- 2 tablespoons fresh lemon juice

- 1 1/2 pounds flank steak
- 1 1/2 tablespoons Worcestershire sauce

DIRECTIONS

1. In a medium bowl, mix the oil, soy sauce, vinegar, lemon juice, Worcestershire sauce, mustard, garlic, and ground black pepper. Place meat in a shallow glass dish. Pour marinade over the steak, turning meat to coat thoroughly. Cover, and refrigerate for 6 hours.
2. Preheat grill for medium-high heat.
3. Oil the grill grate. Place steaks on the grill, and discard the marinade. Grill meat for 5 minutes per side, or to desired doneness.

COTTAGE CHEESE CHICKEN ENCHILADAS

Servings: 6 | Prep: 30m | Cooks: 30m | Total: 1h

NUTRITION FACTS

Calories: 548 | Carbohydrates: 34.4g | Fat: 31.2g | Protein: 33.2g | Cholesterol: 98mg

INGREDIENTS

- 1 tablespoon vegetable oil
- 2 cups cottage cheese
- 2 skinless, boneless chicken breast halves - boiled and shredded
- 1 teaspoon salt
- 1/2 cup chopped onion
- 1 pinch ground black pepper
- 1 (7 ounce) can chopped green chile peppers
- 12 (6 inch) corn tortillas
- 1 (1 ounce) package taco seasoning mix
- 2 cups shredded Monterey Jack cheese
- 1/2 cup sour cream
- 1 (10 ounce) can red enchilada sauce

DIRECTIONS

1. To Make Meat Mixture: Heat oil in medium skillet over medium high heat. Add chicken, onion and green chile peppers and saute until browned, then add taco seasoning and prepare meat mixture according to package directions.
2. To Make Cheese Mixture: In a medium bowl mix sour cream with cottage cheese and season with salt and pepper; stir until well blended.
3. Preheat oven to 350 degrees F (175 degrees C).
4. To Assemble Enchiladas: Heat tortillas until soft. In each tortilla place a spoonful of meat mixture, a spoonful of cheese mixture and a bit of shredded cheese. Roll tortillas and place in a lightly greased

9x13 inch baking dish. Top with any remaining meat and cheese mixture, enchilada sauce and remaining shredded cheese.

5. Bake at 350 degrees F (175 degrees C) for 30 minutes or until cheese is melted and bubbly.

SOUTHWESTERN EGG ROLLS

Servings: 5 | Prep: 20m | Cooks: 15m | Total: 4h32m | Additional: 4h

NUTRITION FACTS

Calories: 419 | Carbohydrates: 21.8g | Fat: 31.2g | Protein: 13.6g | Cholesterol: 29mg

INGREDIENTS

- 2 tablespoons vegetable oil
- 1/2 tablespoon minced fresh parsley
- 1 skinless, boneless chicken breast half
- 1/2 teaspoon ground cumin
- 2 tablespoons minced green onion
- 1/2 teaspoon chili powder
- 2 tablespoons minced red bell pepper
- 1/3 teaspoon salt
- 1/3 cup frozen corn kernels
- 1 pinch ground cayenne pepper
- 1/4 cup black beans, rinsed and drained
- 3/4 cup shredded Monterey Jack cheese
- 2 tablespoons frozen chopped spinach, thawed and drained
- 5 (6 inch) flour tortillas
- 2 tablespoons diced jalapeno peppers
- 1 quart oil for deep frying

DIRECTIONS

1. Rub 1 tablespoon vegetable oil over chicken breast. In a medium saucepan over medium heat, cook chicken approximately 5 minutes per side, until meat is no longer pink and juices run clear. Remove from heat and set aside.

2. Heat remaining 1 tablespoon vegetable oil in a medium saucepan over medium heat. Stir in green onion and red pepper. Cook and stir 5 minutes, until tender.

3. Dice chicken and mix into the pan with onion and red pepper. Mix in corn, black beans, spinach, jalapeno peppers, parsley, cumin, chili powder, salt and cayenne pepper. Cook and stir 5 minutes, until well blended and tender. Remove from heat and stir in Monterey Jack cheese so that it melts.

4. Wrap tortillas with a clean, lightly moist cloth. Microwave on high approximately 1 minute, or until hot and pliable.

5. Spoon even amounts of the mixture into each tortilla. Fold ends of tortillas, then roll tightly around mixture. Secure with toothpicks. Arrange in a medium dish, cover with plastic, and place in the freezer. Freeze at least 4 hours.
6. In a large, deep skillet, heat oil for deep frying to 375 degrees F (190 degrees C). Deep fry frozen, stuffed tortillas 10 minutes each, or until dark golden brown. Drain on paper towels before serving.

TEN MINUTE ENCHILADA SAUCE
Servings: 6 | Prep: 10m | Cooks: 15m | Total: 25m

NUTRITION FACTS

Calories: 116 | Carbohydrates: 7g | Fat: 10.1g | Protein: 1.4g | Cholesterol: 0mg

INGREDIENTS

- 1/4 cup vegetable oil
- 1/4 teaspoon ground cumin
- 2 tablespoons self-rising flour
- 1/4 teaspoon garlic powder
- 1/4 cup New Mexico or California chili powder
- 1/4 teaspoon onion salt
- 1 (8 ounce) can tomato sauce
- salt to taste
- 1 1/2 cups water

DIRECTIONS

1. Combine rice and water in a medium saucepan. Bring to a boil over high heat. Reduce heat to low, cover with lid, and allow to steam until tender, about 20 minutes.
2. While rice is cooking, grind peanuts in a blender and set aside. Heat the margarine in a skillet over medium heat. Stir in the onion; cook and stir until the onion has softened and turned golden brown about 10 minutes. Stir in ginger, carrots, and salt to taste. Reduce heat to low and cover to steam 5 minutes. Stir in cayenne pepper and peanuts. When rice is done, add it to skillet and stir gently to combine with other ingredients. Garnish with chopped cilantro.

CHICKEN ENCHILADAS
Servings: 8 | Prep: 20m | Cooks: 25m | Total: 45m

NUTRITION FACTS

Calories: 352 | Carbohydrates: 30.6g | Fat: 16.9g | Protein: 19.2g | Cholesterol: 50mg

INGREDIENTS

- 1 (10.75 ounce) can condensed cream of chicken soup
- 2 cups chopped cooked chicken breast
- 1/2 cup sour cream
- 1 (4 ounce) can chopped green chile peppers, drained
- 1 tablespoon margarine
- 8 (8 inch) flour tortillas
- 1 onion, chopped
- 1 cup shredded Cheddar cheese
- 1 teaspoon chili powder

DIRECTIONS

1. Preheat oven to 350 degrees F (175 degrees C).
2. In a small bowl mix the soup and sour cream; set aside.
3. Melt margarine in a medium saucepan over medium high heat. Add onion and chili powder, and saute until tender. Stir in the chicken, chile peppers, and 2 tablespoons of the soup mixture. Cook and stir until heated through.
4. Spread 1/2 cup of the soup mixture in a 9x13 inch baking dish. Spoon about 1/4 cup of the chicken mixture down the center of each tortilla. Roll up tortillas, and place, seam-side-down, in the baking dish. Spoon remaining soup mixture on top, and sprinkle with cheese.
5. Bake 25 minutes in the preheated oven, or until bubbly and lightly browned.

SPINACH ENCHILADAS

Servings: 5 | Prep: 20m | Cooks: 20m | Total: 40m

NUTRITION FACTS

Calories: 510 | Carbohydrates: 32.3g | Fat: 36g | Protein: 18.2g | Cholesterol: 95mg

INGREDIENTS

- 1 tablespoon butter
- 1/2 cup sour cream
- 1/2 cup sliced green onions
- 2 cups shredded Monterey Jack cheese
- 2 cloves garlic, minced
- 10 (6 inch) corn tortillas
- 1 (10 ounce) package frozen chopped spinach , thawed, drained and squeezed dry
- 1 (19 ounce) can enchilada sauce
- 1 cup ricotta cheese

DIRECTIONS

1. Preheat the oven to 375 degrees F (190 degrees C).
2. Melt butter in a saucepan over medium heat. Add garlic and onion; cook for a few minutes until fragrant, but not brown. Stir in spinach, and cook for about 5 more minutes. Remove from the heat, and mix in ricotta cheese, sour cream, and 1 cup of Monterey Jack cheese.
3. In a skillet over medium heat, warm tortillas one at a time until flexible, about 15 seconds. Spoon about 1/4 cup of the spinach mixture onto the center of each tortilla. Roll up, and place seam side down in a 9x13 inch baking dish. Pour enchilada sauce over the top, and sprinkle with the remaining cup of Monterey Jack.
4. Bake for 15 to 20 minutes in the preheated oven, until sauce is bubbling and cheese is lightly browned at the edges.

HOMEMADE FLOUR TORTILLAS

Servings: 24 | Prep: 15m | Cooks: 45m | Total: 1h

NUTRITION FACTS

Calories: 86 | Carbohydrates: 16g | Fat: 1.3g | Protein: 2.2g | Cholesterol: 1mg

INGREDIENTS

- 4 cups all-purpose flour
- 2 tablespoons lard
- 1 teaspoon salt
- 1 1/2 cups water
- 2 teaspoons baking powder

DIRECTIONS

1. Whisk the flour, salt, and baking powder together in a mixing bowl. Mix in the lard with your fingers until the flour resembles cornmeal. Add the water and mix until the dough comes together; place on a lightly floured surface and knead a few minutes until smooth and elastic. Divide the dough into 24 equal pieces and roll each piece into a ball.
2. Preheat a large skillet over medium-high heat. Use a well-floured rolling pin to roll a dough ball into a thin, round tortilla. Place into the hot skillet, and cook until bubbly and golden; flip and continue cooking until golden on the other side. Place the cooked tortilla in a tortilla warmer; continue rolling and cooking the remaining dough.

FABULOUS WET BURRITOS

Servings: 6 | Prep: 15m | Cooks: 30m | Total: 45m

NUTRITION FACTS

Calories: 916 | Carbohydrates: 92g | Fat: 42g | Protein: 43.9g | Cholesterol: 122mg

INGREDIENTS

- 1 pound ground beef
- 1 (15 ounce) can chili without beans
- 1/2 cup chopped onion
- 1 (10.75 ounce) can condensed tomato soup
- 1 clove garlic, minced
- 1 (10 ounce) can enchilada sauce
- 1/2 teaspoon cumin
- 6 (12 inch) flour tortillas, warmed
- 1/4 teaspoon salt
- 2 cups shredded lettuce
- 1/8 teaspoon pepper
- 1 cup chopped tomatoes
- 1 (4.5 ounce) can diced green chile peppers
- 2 cups shredded Mexican blend cheese
- 1 (16 ounce) can refried beans
- 1/2 cup chopped green onions

DIRECTIONS

1. Crumble ground beef into a skillet over medium-high heat. Cook and stir until evenly browned. Add onion, and cook until translucent. Drain grease, and season with garlic, cumin, salt and pepper. Stir in the green chilies and refried beans until well blended. Turn off heat, but keep warm.
2. In a saucepan, combine the chili without beans, tomato soup and enchilada sauce. Mix well, and cook over medium heat until heated through. Turn off heat and keep warm.
3. Place a warmed tortilla on a plate, and spoon a generous 1/2 cup of the ground beef mixture onto the center. Top with lettuce and tomato to your liking. Roll up tortilla over the filling. Spoon a generous amount of the sauce over the top, and sprinkle with cheese and green onions. Heat in the microwave for 30 seconds, or until cheese is melted. Repeat with remaining tortillas.

ABSOLUTE MEXICAN CORNBREAD
Servings: 6 | Prep: 15m | Cooks: 1h | Total: 1h15m

NUTRITION FACTS

Calories: 743 | Carbohydrates: 83.6g | Fat: 40.9g | Protein: 14.5g | Cholesterol: 227mg

INGREDIENTS

- 1 cup butter, melted
- 1/2 cup shredded Cheddar cheese
- 1 cup white sugar
- 1 cup all-purpose flour
- 4 eggs
- 1 cup yellow cornmeal

- 1 (15 ounce) can cream-style corn
- 4 teaspoons baking powder
- 1/2 (4 ounce) can chopped green chile peppers, drained
- 1/4 teaspoon salt
- 1/2 cup shredded Monterey Jack cheese

DIRECTIONS

1. Preheat oven to 300 degrees F (150 degrees C). Lightly grease a 9x13 inch baking dish.
2. In a large bowl, beat together butter and sugar. Beat in eggs one at a time. Blend in cream corn, chiles, Monterey Jack and Cheddar cheese.
3. In a separate bowl, stir together flour, cornmeal, baking powder and salt. Add flour mixture to corn mixture; stir until smooth. Pour batter into prepared pan.
4. Bake in preheated oven for 1 hour, until a toothpick inserted into center of the pan comes out clean.

CHIPOTLE CRUSTED PORK TENDERLOIN
Servings: 6 | Prep: 15m | Cooks: 20m | Total: 35m

NUTRITION FACTS

Calories: 183 | Carbohydrates: 11.7g | Fat: 6.1g | Protein: 20.4g | Cholesterol: 62mg

INGREDIENTS

- 1 teaspoon onion powder
- 1 1/2 teaspoons salt
- 1 teaspoon garlic powder
- 4 tablespoons brown sugar
- 3 tablespoons chipotle chile powde
- 2 (3/4 pound) pork tenderloins

DIRECTIONS

1. Preheat grill for medium-high heat.
2. In a large resealable plastic bag, combine the onion powder, garlic powder, chipotle chile powder, salt, and brown sugar. Place tenderloins in bag and shake, coating meat evenly. Refrigerate for 10 to 15 minutes.
3. Lightly oil grill grate, and arrange meat on grate. Cook for 20 minutes, turning meat every 5 minutes. Remove from grill, let stand for 5 to 10 minutes before slicing.

CHARLEY'S SLOW COOKER MEXICAN STYLE MEAT
Servings: 12 | Prep: 30m | Cooks: 8h | Total: 8h50m

NUTRITION FACTS

Calories: 260 | Carbohydrates: 3.3g | Fat: 19.1g | Protein: 18.4g | Cholesterol: 69mg

INGREDIENTS

- 1 (4 pound) chuck roast
- 1 1/4 cups diced green chile pepper
- 1 teaspoon salt
- 1 teaspoon chili powder
- 1 teaspoon ground black pepper
- 1 teaspoon ground cayenne pepper
- 2 tablespoons olive oil
- 1 (5 ounce) bottle hot pepper sauce
- 1 large onion, chopped
- 1 teaspoon garlic powder

DIRECTIONS

1. Trim the roast of any excess fat, and season with salt and pepper. Heat olive oil in a large skillet over medium-high heat. Place the beef in the hot skillet, and brown it quickly on all sides.
2. Transfer the roast to a slow cooker and top it with the chopped onion. Season with chile peppers, chili powder, cayenne pepper, hot pepper sauce, and garlic powder. Add enough water to cover 1/3 of the roast.
3. Cover, and cook on High for 6 hours, checking to make sure there is always at least a small amount of liquid in the bottom of the cooker. Reduce heat to Low, and continue cooking for 2 to 4 hours, or until meat is totally tender and falls apart.
4. Transfer the roast to a bowl and shred it using two forks (reserve 2 cups of cooking liquid, if desired). Serve in tacos or burritos (see Cook's Note).

TAQUERIA STYLE TACOS - CARNE ASADA
Servings: 16 | Prep: 25m | Cooks: 10m | Total: 1h35m

NUTRITION FACTS

Calories: 369 | Carbohydrates: 32.2g | Fat: 19.7g | Protein: 18.1g | Cholesterol: 44mg

INGREDIENTS

- 3 pounds flank steak
- 1 teaspoon paprika
- 1/3 cup white vinegar
- 1 white onion, chopped
- 1/2 cup soy sauce
- 1/2 cup chopped fresh cilantro
- 4 cloves garlic, minced
- 1 lime, juiced

- 2 limes, juiced
- 2 large tomatoes, chopped
- 1/2 cup olive oil
- 2 jalapeno peppers, chopped
- 1 teaspoon salt
- 1 white onion, quartered
- 1 teaspoon ground black pepper
- 4 cloves garlic, peeled
- 1 teaspoon ground white pepper
- 4 dried New Mexico chile pods
- 1 teaspoon garlic powder
- 1 pinch salt and pepper to taste
- 1 teaspoon chili powder
- 1 (32 ounce) package corn tortillas
- 1 teaspoon dried oregano
- 2 cups grated cotija cheese (optional)
- 1 teaspoon ground cumi
- 2 limes, cut into wedges

DIRECTIONS

1. Lay the flank steak in a large glass baking dish. In a medium bowl, whisk together the vinegar, soy sauce, 4 cloves of garlic, juice of two limes, and olive oil. Season with salt, black pepper, white pepper, garlic powder, chili powder, oregano, cumin and paprika. Whisk until well blended, then pour over the steak in the dish. Turn over once to coat both sides. Cover with plastic wrap, and marinate for 1 to 8 hours.
2. In a small bowl, stir together 1 chopped white onion, cilantro, and the juice of 1 lime. Set aside to use as a relish for the tacos.
3. Heat a skillet over medium-high heat. Toast chile pods in the skillet for a few minutes, then remove to a bowl of water to soak for about 30 minutes. Preheat the oven to 450 degrees F (230 degrees C).
4. Place the tomatoes, 1 onion, jalapenos, and 4 cloves of garlic onto a baking sheet. Roast in the oven for about 20 minutes, until toasted but not burnt. Place the roasted vegetables, and soaked chile pods into a blender or food processor, along with salt and pepper. Puree until smooth.
5. Heat vegetable oil in a large skillet over medium-high heat. Cut the marinated flank steak into cubes or strips. Cook, stirring constantly, until the meat is cooked through and most of the liquid has evaporated.
6. Warm the tortillas in a skillet for about a minute on each side to make them pliable. Tortillas may also be warmed in a microwave oven. Arrange two or three tortillas on a plate, and lay a generous amount of beef over them. Top with a sprinkle of the onion relish and a large spoonful of the pureed salsa. Add as much cheese as you like. Garnish with lime wedges, and serve.

POLLO FAJITAS
Servings: 5 | Prep: 15m | Cooks: 10m | Total: 55m | Additional: 30m

NUTRITION FACTS

Calories: 210 | Carbohydrates: 5.7g | Fat: g | Protein: 27.6g | Cholesterol: 113mg

INGREDIENTS

- 1 tablespoon Worcestershire sauce
- 1 1/2 pounds boneless, skinless chicken thighs, cut into strips
- 1 tablespoon cider vinegar
- 1 tablespoon vegetable oil
- 1 tablespoon soy sauce
- 1 onion, thinly sliced
- 1 teaspoon chili powder
- 1 green bell pepper, sliced
- 1 clove garlic, minced
- 1/2 lemon, juiced
- 1 dash hot pepper sauce

DIRECTIONS

1. In a medium bowl, combine Worcestershire sauce, vinegar, soy sauce, chili powder, garlic and hot pepper sauce. Place chicken in sauce, and turn once to coat. Marinate for 30 minutes at room temperature, or cover and refrigerate for several hours.
2. Heat oil in a large skillet over high heat. Add chicken strips to the pan, and saute for 5 minutes. Add the onion and green pepper, and saute another 3 minutes. Remove from heat, and sprinkle with lemon juice.

EASY CHICKEN ENCHILADAS
Servings: 6 | Prep: 20m | Cooks: 30m | Total: 50m

NUTRITION FACTS

Calories: 565 | Carbohydrates: 32.8g | Fat: 34.1g | Protein: 32.6g | Cholesterol: 120mg

INGREDIENTS

- 1 (8 ounce) package cream cheese
- 1 (15.5 ounce) can pinto beans, drained
- 1 cup salsa
- 6 (6 inch) flour tortillas
- 2 cups chopped cooked chicken breast meat
- 2 cups shredded Colby-Jack cheese

DIRECTIONS

1. Preheat the oven to 350 degrees F (175 degrees C). Lightly grease a 9x13 inch baking dish.
2. In a small saucepan over medium heat, combine the cream cheese and salsa. Cook, stirring until melted and well blended. Stir in chicken and pinto beans. Fill tortillas with the mixture, roll and place into the prepared baking dish. Spread cheese over the top. Cover with aluminum foil.
3. Bake for 30 minutes, or until heated through. Garnish with your favorite toppings such as lettuce and tomatoes, or sour cream.

BEEF AND BEAN CHIMICHANGAS
Servings: 8 | Prep: 15m | Cooks: 30m | Total: 45m

NUTRITION FACTS

Calories: 821 | Carbohydrates: 83.6g | Fat: 36g | Protein: 40.1g | Cholesterol: 97mg

INGREDIENTS

- 1 pound lean ground beef
- 1 teaspoon ground cumin
- 3/4 cup chopped onion
- 1 (16 ounce) can refried beans
- 3/4 cup diced green bell pepper
- 8 (12 inch) flour tortillas
- 1 1/2 cups whole kernel corn
- 1 (16 ounce) package shredded Monterey Jack cheese
- 2 cups taco sauce
- 1 tablespoon butter, melted
- 2 teaspoons chili powder
- shredded lettuce
- 1 teaspoon garlic salt
- 1 tomato, diced

DIRECTIONS

1. Preheat the oven to 350 degrees F (175 degrees C).
2. Brown the ground beef in a skillet over medium-high heat. Drain excess grease, and add the onion, bell pepper, and corn. Cook for about 5 more minutes, or until vegetables are tender. Stir in the taco sauce, and season with chili powder, garlic salt and cumin, stirring until blended. Cook until heated through, then remove from heat, and set aside.
3. Open the can of beans, and spread a thin layer of beans onto each of the tortillas. Spoon the beef mixture down the center, and then top with as much shredded cheese as you like. Roll up the tortillas, and place them seam-side down onto a baking sheet. Brush the tortillas with melted butter.
4. Bake for 30 to 35 minutes in the preheated oven, or until golden brown. Serve with lettuce and tomato.

D'S FAMOUS SALSA

Servings: 16 | Prep: 10m | Cooks: 0m | Total: 10m

NUTRITION FACTS

Calories: 16 | Carbohydrates: 3.9g | Fat: 0.1g | Protein: 0.6g | Cholesterol: 0mg

INGREDIENTS

- 2 (14.5 ounce) cans stewed tomatoes
- 1 teaspoon salt
- 1/2 onion, finely diced
- 1/4 cup canned sliced green chiles, or to taste
- 1 teaspoon minced garlic
- 3 tablespoons chopped fresh cilantro
- 1/2 lime, juiced

DIRECTIONS

1. Place the tomatoes, onion, garlic, lime juice, salt, green chiles, and cilantro in a blender or food processor. Blend on low to desired consistency.

CHICKEN QUESADILLAS

Servings: 20 | Prep: 30m | Cooks: 25m | Total: 55m

NUTRITION FACTS

Calories: 244 | Carbohydrates: 21.8g | Fat: 11.3g | Protein: 13.7g | Cholesterol: 35mg

INGREDIENTS

- 1 pound skinless, boneless chicken breast, diced
- 1 onion, chopped
- 1 (1.27 ounce) packet fajita seasoning
- 10 (10 inch) flour tortillas
- 1 tablespoon vegetable oil
- 1 (8 ounce) package shredded Cheddar cheese
- 2 green bell peppers, chopped
- 1 tablespoon bacon bits
- 2 red bell peppers, chopped
- 1 (8 ounce) package shredded Monterey Jack cheese

DIRECTIONS

1. Preheat the broiler. Grease a baking sheet.
2. Toss the chicken with the fajita seasoning, then spread onto the baking sheet. Place under the broiler and cook until the chicken pieces are no longer pink in the center, about 5 minutes.
3. Preheat oven to 350 degrees F (175 degrees C).
4. Heat the oil in a large saucepan over medium heat. Stir in the green bell peppers, red bell peppers, onion, and chicken. Cook and stir until the vegetables have softened, about 10 minutes.
5. Layer half of each tortilla with the chicken and vegetable mixture, then sprinkle with the Cheddar cheese, bacon bits, and Monterey Jack. Fold the tortillas in half and Place onto a baking sheet.
6. Bake quesadillas in the preheated oven until the cheeses have melted, about 10 minutes.

MEXICAN RICE
Servings: 6 | Prep: 5m | Cooks: 25m | Total: 30m

NUTRITION FACTS

Calories: 158 | Carbohydrates: 29.1g | Fat: 2.8g | Protein: 3.4g | Cholesterol: 1mg

INGREDIENTS

*   1 cup long grain white rice
*   1 tomato, seeded and chopped
*   1 tablespoon vegetable oil
*   1 cube chicken bouillon
*   1 1/2 cups chicken broth
*   salt and pepper to taste
*   1/2 onion, finely chopped
*   1/2 teaspoon ground cumin
*   1/2 green bell pepper, finely chopped
*   1/2 cup chopped fresh cilantro
*   1 fresh jalapeno pepper, chopped
*   1 clove garlic, halved

DIRECTIONS

1. In a medium sauce pan, cook rice in oil over medium heat for about 3 minutes. Pour in chicken broth, and bring to a boil. Stir in onion, green pepper, jalapeno, and diced tomato. Season with bouillon cube, salt and pepper, cumin, cilantro, and garlic. Bring to a boil, cover, and reduce heat to low. Cook for 20 minutes.

GRILLED FISH TACOS WITH CHIPOTLE-LIME DRESSING
Servings: 6 | Prep: 35m | Cooks: 9m | Total: 6h44m

NUTRITION FACTS

Calories: 416 | Carbohydrates: 38.5g | Fat: 19.2g | Protein: 19.2g | Cholesterol: 43mg

INGREDIENTS

- 1/4 cup extra virgin olive oil
- 1/2 cup adobo sauce from chipotle peppers
- 2 tablespoons distilled white vinegar
- 2 tablespoons fresh lime juice
- 2 tablespoons fresh lime juice
- 2 teaspoons lime zest
- 2 teaspoons lime zest
- 1/4 teaspoon cumin
- 1 1/2 teaspoons honey
- 1/4 teaspoon chili powder
- 2 cloves garlic, minced
- 1/2 teaspoon seafood seasoning, such as Old Bay™
- 1/2 teaspoon cumin
- salt and pepper to taste
- 1/2 teaspoon chili powder
- 1 (10 ounce) package tortillas
- 1 teaspoon seafood seasoning, such as Old Bay™
- 3 ripe tomatoes, seeded and diced
- 1/2 teaspoon ground black pepper
- 1 bunch cilantro, chopped
- 1 teaspoon hot pepper sauce, or to taste
- 1 small head cabbage, cored and shredded
- 1 pound tilapia fillets, cut into chunks
- 2 limes, cut in wedges
- 1 (8 ounce) container light sour cream

DIRECTIONS

1. To make the marinade, whisk together the olive oil, vinegar, lime juice, lime zest, honey, garlic, cumin, chili powder, seafood seasoning, black pepper, and hot sauce in a bowl until blended. Place the tilapia in a shallow dish, and pour the marinade over the fish. Cover, and refrigerate 6 to 8 hours.
2. To make the dressing, combine the sour cream and adobo sauce in a bowl. Stir in the lime juice, lime zest, cumin, chili powder, seafood seasoning. Add salt, and pepper in desired amounts. Cover, and refrigerate until needed.
3. Preheat an outdoor grill for high heat and lightly oil grate. Set grate 4 inches from the heat.
4. Remove fish from marinade, drain off any excess and discard marinade. Grill fish pieces until easily flaked with a fork, turning once, about 9 minutes.
5. Assemble tacos by placing fish pieces in the center of tortillas with desired amounts of tomatoes, cilantro, and cabbage; drizzle with dressing. To serve, roll up tortillas around fillings, and garnish with lime wedges.

CHILI RELLENOS CASSEROLE
Servings: 6 | Prep: 15m | Cooks:45 m | Total: 1h

NUTRITION FACTS

Calories: 387 | Carbohydrates: 12g | Fat: 27.6g | Protein: 23.9g | Cholesterol: 140mg

INGREDIENTS

- 2 (7 ounce) cans whole green chile peppers, drained
- 8 ounces Monterey Jack cheese, shredded
- 8 ounces Longhorn or Cheddar cheese, shredded
- 2 eggs, beaten

DIRECTIONS

1. Preheat oven to 350 degrees F (175 degrees C). Spray a 9x13-inch baking dish with cooking spray.
2. Lay half of the chilies evenly in bottom of baking dish. Sprinkle with half of the Jack and Cheddar cheeses, and cover with remaining chilies. In a bowl, mix together the eggs, milk, and flour, and pour over the top of the chilies.
3. Bake in the preheated oven for 25 minutes. Remove from oven, pour tomato sauce evenly over the top, and continue baking another 15 minutes. Sprinkle with remaining Jack and Cheddar cheeses, and serve.

TERRIFIC TURKEY CHILI
Servings: 6 | Prep: 15m | Cooks: 55m | Total: 1h10m

NUTRITION FACTS

Calories: 506 | Carbohydrates: 24.1g | Fat: 31.9g | Protein: 34.7g | Cholesterol: 125mg

INGREDIENTS

- 3 tablespoons vegetable oil, divided
- 1 (14.5 ounce) can crushed tomatoes, or coarsely chopped tomatoes packed in puree
- 1 1/2 pounds ground turkey
- 1 (7 ounce) can chopped green chile peppers
- 1 (1 ounce) package taco seasoning mix
- 1 medium onion, finely chopped
- 1 teaspoon ground coriander
- 1 green bell pepper, diced
- 1 teaspoon dried oregano
- 3 medium zucchini, halved lengthwise and sliced
- 1 teaspoon chili pepper flakes

- 1 bunch green onions, chopped
- 2 tablespoons tomato paste
- 1 cup sour cream
- 1 (14.5 ounce) can beef broth
- 1 cup shredded Cheddar cheese
- 1 (7 ounce) can salsa

DIRECTIONS

1. Heat 1 tablespoon of oil in a large stock pot over medium-high heat. Crumble turkey into the pot, stirring with a wooden spoon to break apart as much as possible. Season with taco seasoning mix, coriander, oregano, chili flakes, and tomato paste, and mix until meat is evenly coated with seasonings. Continue cooking, reducing heat if necessary, until turkey is well browned.
2. Pour in beef broth, and simmer to reduce liquid slightly, about 5 minutes. Add salsa, tomatoes, and green chilies, and continue cooking at a moderate simmer for ten minutes. Adjust the thickness at any time you feel necessary by adding water.
3. While chili is still cooking, heat one tablespoon of oil in a large skillet over medium-high heat. Cook onion and green bell pepper, stirring occasionally for 5 minutes, or until onion is translucent and bell pepper is lightly browned. Add onion and bell pepper to the chili, and continue cooking at a very low simmer.
4. In the same skillet, heat the remaining tablespoon of oil over medium-high heat. Add the zucchini, and cook stirring occasionally, for 5 minutes, or until lightly browned. Add the zucchini to the chili, reduce heat, and continue cooking 15 minutes more. Again, adjust the consistency with water as needed.
5. Ladle chili into serving bowls. Top with sour cream, green onion, and cheddar cheese, and serve.

MEXICAN CASSEROLE
Servings: 5 | Prep: 15m | Cooks: 15m | Total: 30m

NUTRITION FACTS

Calories: 384 | Carbohydrates: 34g | Fat: 16.6g | Protein: 26.8g | Cholesterol: 59mg

INGREDIENTS

- 2 tablespoons vegetable oil
- 1/4 cup salsa
- 3/4 pound cubed skinless, boneless chicken breast meat
- water as needed
- 1/2 (1.25 ounce) package taco seasoning mix
- 1 cup shredded Mexican-style cheese
- 1 (15 ounce) can black beans, rinsed and drained
- 1v1/2 cups crushed plain tortilla chips
- 1 (8.75 ounce) can sweet corn, drained

DIRECTIONS

1. In a large skillet over medium high heat, saute chicken in oil until cooked through and no longer pink inside. Add taco seasoning, beans, corn, salsa and a little water to prevent drying out. Cover skillet and simmer over medium low heat for 10 minutes.
2. Preheat oven to 350 degrees F (175 degrees C).
3. Transfer chicken mixture to a 9x13 inch baking dish. Top with 1/2 cup of the cheese and crushed tortilla chips.
4. Bake in the preheated oven for 15 minutes. Add remaining 1/2 cup cheese and bake until cheese is melted and bubbly.

BEEF ENCHILADAS

Servings: 10 | Prep: 25m | Cooks: 20m | Total: 45m

NUTRITION FACTS

Calories: 448 | Carbohydrates: 40.5g | Fat: 21.1g | Protein: 22.2g | Cholesterol: 60mg

INGREDIENTS

- 1 pound lean ground beef
- 10 (10 inch) flour tortillas
- 1 small onion, chopped
- 2 cups shredded Cheddar cheese
- 1 (1.5 ounce) package dry enchilada sauce mix
- 1 (2.25 ounce) can sliced black olives, drained

DIRECTIONS

1. Preheat oven to 350 degrees F (175 degrees C). In a medium skillet over medium high heat, cook the ground beef and onion until beef is evenly browned and onion is tender.
2. Prepare the enchilada sauce according to package directions. Pour 1/4 cup of the sauce into the bottom of a 9x13 inch baking dish.
3. On each flour tortilla, place an equal portion of the ground beef mixture and about 1 ounce of Cheddar cheese, reserving at least 1/2 cup of cheese. Then tightly roll the tortillas and place seam side down in the baking dish.
4. Pour the remaining sauce over the top of the enchiladas and sprinkle with the remaining cheese and olives.
5. Bake in a preheated oven for 20 minutes, or until the sauce is bubbly and cheese is thoroughly melted.

AMY'S CILANTRO CREAM SAUCE

Servings: 4 | Prep: 10m | Cooks: 0m | Total: 10m

NUTRITION FACTS

Calories: 230 | Carbohydrates: 7.1g | Fat: 20.5g | Protein: 5g | Cholesterol: 63mg

INGREDIENTS

- 1 (8 ounce) package cream cheese, softened
- 1/2 teaspoon ground cumin
- 1 tablespoon sour cream
- 2 teaspoons garlic powder
- 1 (7 ounce) can tomatillo salsa
- 1 bunch fresh cilantro, chopped
- 1 teaspoon freshly ground black pepper
- 1 tablespoon fresh lime juice
- 1 teaspoon celery salt

DIRECTIONS

1. Combine cream cheese, sour cream, salsa, pepper, celery salt, cumin, garlic powder, cilantro and lime juice in a blender or food processor. Blend until smooth and creamy. Place in a serving bowl.

TACOS IN PASTA SHELLS
Servings: 6 | Prep: 30m | Cooks: 30m | Total: 1h

NUTRITION FACTS

Calories: 735 | Carbohydrates: 47.6g | Fat: 44.2g | Protein: 35.7g | Cholesterol: 136mg

INGREDIENTS

- 1 1/4 pounds lean ground beef
- 1 cup taco sauce
- 1 (3 ounce) package cream cheese
- 1 cup shredded Cheddar cheese
- 1 teaspoon salt
- 1 cup shredded Monterey Jack cheese
- 1 teaspoon chili powder
- 1 1/2 cups crushed tortilla chips
- 18 jumbo pasta shells
- 1 cup sour cream
- 2 tablespoons butter, melted

DIRECTIONS

1. In a large skillet, brown beef over medium heat until no longer pink; drain. Add cream cheese, salt and chili powder; mix and simmer for 5 minutes.
2. Meanwhile, bring a large pot of lightly salted water to a boil. Add pasta and cook for 8 to 10 minutes or until al dente; drain. Toss cooked shells in butter.
3. Preheat oven to 350 degrees F (175 degrees C).
4. Fill shells with beef mixture and arrange in a 9x13 inch baking dish; pour taco sauce over shells. Cover with foil and bake in preheated oven for 15 minutes.
5. Remove dish from oven and top with Cheddar cheese, Monterey Jack cheese and tortilla chips; return dish to oven to cook for 15 minutes more.
6. Top with sour cream and onions; serve.

MEXICAN BAKED FISH
Servings: 6 | Prep: 15m | Cooks: 15m | Total: 30m

NUTRITION FACTS

Calories: 311 | Carbohydrates: 11.3g | Fat: 17.6g | Protein: 27.6g | Cholesterol: 69mg

INGREDIENTS

- 1 1/2 pounds cod
- 1/2 cup coarsely crushed corn chips
- 1 cup salsa
- 1 avocado - peeled, pitted and sliced
- 1 cup shredded sharp Cheddar cheese
- 1/4 cup sour cream

DIRECTIONS

1. Preheat oven to 400 degrees F (200 degrees C). Lightly grease one 8x12 inch baking dish.
2. Rinse fish fillets under cold water, and pat dry with paper towels. Lay fillets side by side in the prepared baking dish. Pour the salsa over the top, and sprinkle evenly with the shredded cheese. Top with the crushed corn chips.
3. Bake, uncovered, in the preheated oven for 15 minutes, or until fish is opaque and flakes with a fork. Serve topped with sliced avocado and sour cream.

GROUND BEEF ENCHILADAS
Servings: 6 | Prep: 15m | Cooks: 40m | Total: 55m

NUTRITION FACTS

Calories: 556 | Carbohydrates: 26.1g | Fat: 33.8g | Protein: 34.8g | Cholesterol: 116mg

INGREDIENTS

- 1 1/2 pounds lean ground beef

- 1 cup plain yogurt
- 1 bunch green onions, finely chopped
- 1 (10.75 ounce) can condensed cream of chicken soup
- 1 diced fresh jalapeno pepper, or to taste
- 2 cups shredded mozzarella cheese
- 1/4 cup water
- 6 (6 inch) corn tortillas
- 1 (1.25 ounce) package taco seasoning mix

DIRECTIONS

1. Preheat oven to 350 degrees F (175 degrees C).
2. In a large skillet over medium heat, cook the ground beef, green onion, and jalapeno pepper until the beef is evenly brown. Stir in water and taco seasoning. Simmer until water has evaporated.
3. In a medium bowl, mix together yogurt, condensed soup, and cheese.
4. Divide the meat mixture evenly between tortillas. Place a couple of tablespoons of cheese mixture over meat, and roll up. Place in a 7x11 inch baking dish. Repeat for each tortilla. Spoon remaining cheese mixture over the top of the tortillas.
5. Bake in preheated oven for 20 to 30 minutes.

EASY GUACAMOLE
Servings: 16 | Prep: 10m | Cooks: 30m | Total: 40m

NUTRITION FACTS

Calories: 45 | Carbohydrates: 3.4g | Fat: 3.7g | Protein: 0.7g | Cholesterol: 0mg

INGREDIENTS

- 2 avocados
- 1 ripe tomato, chopped
- 1 small onion, finely chopped
- 1 lime, juiced
- 1 clove garlic, minced
- salt and pepper to taste

DIRECTIONS

1. Peel and mash avocados in a medium serving bowl. Stir in onion, garlic, tomato, lime juice, salt and pepper. Season with remaining lime juice and salt and pepper to taste. Chill for half an hour to blend flavors.

PICO DE GALLO CHICKEN QUESADILLAS
Servings: 4 | Prep: 25m | Cooks: 30m | Total: 55m

NUTRITION FACTS

Calories: 673 | Carbohydrates: 72.8g | Fat: 29.1g | Protein: 31g | Cholesterol: 65mg

INGREDIENTS

- 2 tomatoes, diced
- 2 skinless, boneless chicken breast halves - cut into strips
- 1 onion, finely chopped
- 1/2 onion, thinly sliced
- 2 limes, juiced
- 1 green bell pepper, thinly sliced
- 2 tablespoons chopped fresh cilantro
- 2 cloves garlic, minced
- 1 jalapeno pepper, seeded and minced
- 4 (12 inch) flour tortillas
- salt and pepper to taste
- 1 cup shredded Monterey Jack cheese
- 2 tablespoons olive oil, divided
- 1/4 cup sour cream, for topping

DIRECTIONS

1. In a small bowl, combine tomatoes, onion, lime juice, cilantro, jalapeno, salt, and pepper. Set pico de gallo aside.
2. In a large skillet, heat 1 tablespoon olive oil. Add chicken and saute until cooked through and juices run clear. Remove chicken from skillet and set aside.
3. Put the remaining 1 tablespoon of olive oil in the hot skillet and saute the sliced onion and green pepper until tender. Stir in the minced garlic and saute until the aroma is strong. Mix in half of the pico de gallo and chicken breast meat. Set aside; keep warm.
4. In a heavy skillet, heat one flour tortilla. Spread 1/4 cup shredded cheese on the tortilla and top with 1/2 the chicken mixture. Sprinkle another 1/4 cup cheese over the chicken and top with another tortilla. When bottom tortilla is lightly brown and cheese has started to melt, flip quesadilla and cook on the opposite side. Remove quesadilla from skillet and cut into quarters. Repeat with remaining ingredients. Serve quesadillas with sour cream and remaining pico de gallo.

QUICK AND EASY GREEN CHILE CHICKEN ENCHILADA CASSEROLE

Servings: 8 | Prep: 30m | Cooks: 1h30m | Total: 2h

Calories: 488 | Carbohydrates: 32.6g | Fat: 25.2g | Protein: 33.1g | Cholesterol: 95mg

INGREDIENTS

- 4 skinless, boneless chicken breast halves
- 1 (28 ounce) can green chile enchilada sauce
- garlic salt to taste
- 1 (16 ounce) package shredded Monterey Jack cheese
- 18 (6 inch) corn tortillas, torn in half
- 1 (8 ounce) container reduced fat sour cream

DIRECTIONS

1. Preheat oven to 350 degrees F (175 degrees C). Lightly grease a medium baking dish.
2. Season chicken with garlic salt. Arrange in the prepared baking dish. Bake 45 minutes in the preheated oven, until no longer pink and juices run clear. Cool, shred, and set aside.
3. With metal tongs, char each tortilla half over the open flame of a gas stove burner for about 1 minute, until lightly puffed.
4. Pour about 1/2 inch enchilada sauce in the bottom of a medium baking dish, and arrange 6 tortillas in a single layer. Top with 1/2 the chicken, 1/3 cheese, 1/2 the sour cream, and 1/3 of the remaining enchilada sauce. Repeat. Coat remaining tortillas thoroughly with remaining enchilada sauce, and arrange on top of the layers. Sprinkle with remaining cheese, and top with any remaining enchilada sauce
5. Cover, and bake 45 minutes in the preheated oven. Cool slightly before serving.

BEEF NACHO CASSEROLE
Servings: 6 | Prep: 15m | Cooks: 20m | Total: 35m

NUTRITION FACTS

Calories: 497 | Carbohydrates: 23.6g | Fat: 33.6g | Protein: 26.1g | Cholesterol: 98mg

INGREDIENTS

- 1 pound ground beef
- 1 teaspoon chili powder
- 1 1/2 cups chunky salsa
- 2 cups crushed tortilla chips
- 1 (10 ounce) can whole kernel corn, drained
- 2 cups Colby cheese
- 3/4 cup creamy salad dressing (e.g. Miracle Whip)

DIRECTIONS

1. Preheat the oven to 350 degrees F (175 degrees C).
2. Place ground beef in a large skillet over medium-high heat. Cook, stirring to crumble, until evenly browned. Drain grease. Remove from the heat, and stir the salsa, corn, mayonnaise and chili powder into the beef. In a 2 quart casserole dish, layer the ground beef mixture, tortilla chips and cheese twice, ending with cheese on top.
3. Bake for 20 minutes uncovered in the preheated oven, until cheese is melted and dish is thoroughly heated.

FIERY FISH TACOS WITH CRUNCHY CORN SALSA
Servings: 6 | Prep: 30m | Cooks: 10m | Total: 40m

NUTRITION FACTS

Calories: 351 | Carbohydrates: 40.3g | Fat: 9.6g | Protein: 28.7g | Cholesterol: 43mg

INGREDIENTS

- 2 cups cooked corn kernels
- 1 tablespoon ground black pepper
- 1/2 cup diced red onion
- 2 tablespoons salt, or to taste
- 1 cup peeled, diced jicama
- 6 (4 ounce) fillets tilapia
- 1/2 cup diced red bell pepper
- 2 tablespoons olive oil
- 1 cup fresh cilantro leaves, chopped
- 12 corn tortillas, warmed
- 1 lime, juiced and zested
- 2 tablespoons sour cream, or to taste
- 2 tablespoons cayenne pepper, or to taste

DIRECTIONS

1. Preheat grill for high heat.
2. In a medium bowl, mix together corn, red onion, jicama, red bell pepper, and cilantro. Stir in lime juice and zest.
3. In a small bowl, combine cayenne pepper, ground black pepper, and salt.
4. Brush each fillet with olive oil, and sprinkle with spices to taste.
5. Arrange fillets on grill grate, and cook for 3 minutes per side. For each fiery fish taco, top two corn tortillas with fish, sour cream, and corn salsa.

SLOW COOKER ENCHILADAS

Servings: 6 | Prep: 20m | Cooks: 45m | Total: 1h5m

NUTRITION FACTS

Calories: 712 | Carbohydrates: 36g | Fat: 45.6g | Protein: 40.9g | Cholesterol: 142mg

INGREDIENTS

- 1 pound lean ground beef
- 1 (12 ounce) jar chunky salsa
- 10 (6 inch) corn tortillas, quartered
- 1 (10.75 ounce) can condensed cream of mushroom soup
- 1 (1 ounce) package taco seasoning mix
- 1 (10.75 ounce) can condensed cream of chicken soup
- 1 1/4 cups water
- 4 cups shredded Mexican cheese blend

DIRECTIONS

1. Crumble the ground beef into a skillet over medium-high heat. Cook and stir until evenly browned. Add taco seasoning and water; simmer for 15 minutes over low heat.
2. In a medium bowl, stir together the salsa, cream of mushroom soup and cream of chicken soup. Mix in most of the cheese, reserving 3/4 cup for later.
3. Place a layer of tortillas covering the bottom of a slow cooker. Scoop a layer of the ground beef over that, and then spoon a layer of the cheese mixture. Repeat the layers until you run out of stuff, ending with a layer of tortillas on the top. Top with remaining cheese.
4. Cover, and cook on High for 45 minutes to 1 hour.

RED ENCHILADA SAUCE

Servings: 8 | Prep: 5m | Cooks: 15m | Total: 20m

NUTRITION FACTS

Calories: 27 | Carbohydrates: 2.5g | Fat: 1.9g | Protein: 0.7g | Cholesterol: 0mg

INGREDIENTS

- 1 tablespoon olive oil
- 1/8 teaspoon salt
- 2 cloves garlic, minced
- 1/4 teaspoon ground cumin
- 1 teaspoon minced onion
- 1 teaspoon dried parsley
- 1/2 teaspoon dried oregano

- 1/4 cup salsa
- 2 1/2 teaspoons chili powder
- 1 (6 ounce) can tomato sauce
- 1/2 teaspoon dried basil
- 1 1/2 cups water
- 1/8 teaspoon ground black pepper

DIRECTIONS

1. Heat the oil in a large saucepan over medium heat. Add the garlic and saute for 1 to 2 minutes. Add the onion, oregano, chili powder, basil, ground black pepper, salt, cumin, parsley, salsa and tomato sauce.
2. Mix together and then stir in the water. Bring to a boil, reduce heat to low and simmer for 15 to 20 minutes.

SALSA CHICKEN BURRITO FILLING
Servings: 4 | Prep: 5m | Cooks: 30m | Total: 35m

NUTRITION FACTS

Calories: 107 | Carbohydrates: 9.6g | Fat: 1.5g | Protein: 12.3g | Cholesterol. 30mg

INGREDIENTS

- 2 skinless, boneless chicken breast halves
- 1 teaspoon ground cumin
- 1 (4 ounce) can tomato sauce
- 2 cloves garlic, minced
- 1/4 cup salsa
- 1 teaspoon chili powder
- 1 (1.25 ounce) package taco seasoning mix
- hot sauce to taste

DIRECTIONS

1. Place chicken breasts and tomato sauce in a medium saucepan over medium high heat. Bring to a boil, then add the salsa, seasoning, cumin, garlic and chili powder. Let simmer for 15 minutes.
2. With a fork, start pulling the chicken meat apart into thin strings. Keep cooking pulled chicken meat and sauce, covered, for another 5 to 10 minutes. Add hot sauce to taste and stir together (Note: You may need to add a bit of water if the mixture is cooked too high and gets too thick.)

QUICK AND EASY MEXICAN CHICKEN
Servings: 4 | Prep: 15m | Cooks: 25m | Total: 40m

NUTRITION FACTS

Calories: 264 | Carbohydrates: 4.9g | Fat: 11.1g | Protein: 35.4g | Cholesterol: 98mg

INGREDIENTS

- 4 skinless, boneless chicken breasts
- 1 pinch ground black pepper
- cooking spray
- 1 pinch ground cumin
- 1 clove garlic, minced
- 1 cup salsa
- 1 pinch salt
- 1 cup shredded Cheddar cheese

DIRECTIONS

1. Preheat oven to 375 degrees F (190 degrees C).
2. Heat a greased skillet to medium. Rub chicken pieces with garlic, salt, pepper and cumin to taste; place in hot skillet. Cook until brown on both sides and no longer pink, 10 to 15 minutes.
3. Transfer chicken to 9x13-inch baking dish or casserole dish, top with salsa and cheese, and bake in preheated oven until cheese is bubbly and starts to brown, 15 to 20 minutes.

SEVEN LAYER TORTILLA PIE
Servings: 6 | Prep: 15m | Cooks: 40m | Total: 55m

NUTRITION FACTS

Calories: 405 | Carbohydrates: 54.8g | Fat: 11.7g | Protein: 21.1g | Cholesterol: 16mg

INGREDIENTS

- 2 (15 ounce) cans pinto beans, drained and rinsed
- 1/2 cup chopped tomatoes
- 1 cup salsa, divided
- 7 (8 inch) flour tortillas
- 2 cloves garlic, minced
- 2 cups shredded reduced-fat Cheddar cheese
- 2 tablespoons chopped fresh cilantro
- 1 cup salsa
- 1 (15 ounce) can black beans, rinsed and drained
- 1/2 cup sour cream

DIRECTIONS

1. Preheat oven to 400 degrees F (200 degrees C).
2. In a large bowl, mash pinto beans. Stir in 3/4 cup salsa and garlic.
3. In a separate bowl, mix together 1/4 cup salsa, cilantro, black beans and tomatoes.
4. Place 1 tortilla in a pie plate or tart dish. Spread 3/4 cup pinto bean mixture over tortilla to within 1/2 inch of edge. Top with 1/4 cup cheese, and cover with another tortilla. Spread with 2/3 cup black bean mixture, and top with 1/4 cup cheese. Repeat layering twice. Cover with remaining tortilla, and spread with remaining pinto bean mixture and cheese.
5. Cover with foil, and bake in preheated oven for about 40 minutes. Cut into wedges, and serve with salsa and sour cream.

APPLE ENCHILADA DESSERT

Servings: 6 | Prep: 15m | Cooks: 20m | Total: 35m

NUTRITION FACTS

Calories: 484 | Carbohydrates: 88.3g | Fat: 13.5g | Protein: 4.5g | Cholesterol: 0mg

INGREDIENTS

- 1 (21 ounce) can apple pie filling
- 1/2 cup white sugar
- 6 (8 inch) flour tortillas
- 1/2 cup packed brown sugar
- 1 teaspoon ground cinnamon
- 1/2 cup water
- 1/3 cup margarine

DIRECTIONS

1. Preheat oven to 350 degrees F (175 degrees C).
2. Spoon fruit evenly onto all tortillas, sprinkle with cinnamon. Roll up tortillas and place seam side down on lightly greased 8x8 baking pan.
3. Bring margarine, sugars and water to a boil in a medium sauce pan. Reduce heat and simmer, stirring constantly for 3 minutes.
4. Pour sauce evenly over tortillas; sprinkle with extra cinnamon on top if desired. Bake in preheated oven for 20 minutes.
5. Makes 6 large tortillas; may be cut in half to serve 12.

LAYERED CHICKEN AND BLACK BEAN ENCHILADA CASSEROLE

Servings: 8 | Prep: 25m | Cooks: 45m | Total: 1h10m

NUTRITION FACTS

Calories: 366 | Carbohydrates: 16.4g | Fat: 23.7g | Protein: 23g | Cholesterol: 92mg

INGREDIENTS

- 2 cups diced chicken breast meat
- 1 (4.5 ounce) can diced green chile peppers, drained
- 1/2 teaspoon ground cumin
- 1 (10 ounce) can red enchilada sauce
- 1/2 teaspoon ground coriander
- 8 (6 inch) corn tortillas
- 2 tablespoons chopped fresh cilantro
- 2 cups shredded Mexican blend cheese
- 1 (15 ounce) can black beans, rinsed and drained
- 1 (8 ounce) container sour cream

DIRECTIONS

1. Preheat the oven to 375 degrees F (190 degrees C).
2. Heat a large skillet over medium heat, and spray with vegetable cooking spray. Saute chicken with cumin and coriander until chicken is cooked through. Transfer to a medium bowl. Stir in the cilantro, black beans, and green chile peppers.
3. Spread half of the enchilada sauce over the bottom of an 11x7 inch baking dish. Place 4 tortillas over the sauce, overlapping if necessary. Spoon half of the chicken mixture over the tortillas, and sprinkle with half of the cheese and half of the sour cream. Spoon the remaining enchilada sauce over the cheese, and make another layer of tortillas. Layer the remaining chicken mixture over the tortillas. Cover dish with a lid or aluminum foil.
4. Bake for 30 minutes in the preheated oven. Remove the cover, and sprinkle the remaining cheese over the top and dot with sour cream. Continue cooking, uncovered, for an additional 5 to 10 minutes, or until cheese melts. Let stand 10 minutes before serving.

BEST BLACK BEANS

Servings: 4 | Prep: 10m | Cooks: 5m | Total: 15m

NUTRITION FACTS

Calories: 112 | Carbohydrates: 20.8g | Fat: 0.4g | Protein: 7.1g | Cholesterol: 0mg

INGREDIENTS

- 1 (16 ounce) can black beans
- 1 tablespoon chopped fresh cilantro
- 1 small onion, chopped
- 1/4 teaspoon cayenne pepper
- 1 clove garlic, chopped
- salt to taste

DIRECTIONS

1. In a medium saucepan, combine beans, onion, and garlic, and bring to a boil. Reduce heat to medium-low. Season with cilantro, cayenne, and salt. Simmer for 5 minutes, and serve.

OUTRAGEOUS WARM CHICKEN NACHO DIP
Servings: 12 | Prep: 20m | Cooks: 1h15m | Total: 1h35m

NUTRITION FACTS

Calories: 232 | Carbohydrates: 8.7g | Fat: 13.6g | Protein: 18.6g | Cholesterol: 60mg

INGREDIENTS

- 1 (14 ounce) can diced tomatoes with green chile peppers (such as RO*TEL), drained
- 1/4 cup diced green onion
- 1 (1 pound) loaf processed cheese food (such as Velveeta), cubed
- 1 1/2 tablespoons taco seasoning mix
- 2 large cooked skinless, boneless chicken breast halves, shredded
- 2 tablespoons minced jalapeno pepper, or to taste (optional)
- 1/3 cup sour cream
- 1 cup black beans, rinsed and drained

DIRECTIONS

1. Place the diced tomatoes, processed cheese, chicken meat, sour cream, green onion, taco seasoning, and jalapeno pepper into a slow cooker. Cook on High, stirring occasionally until the cheese has melted and the dip is hot, 1 to 2 hours. Stir in the black beans, and cook 15 more minutes to reheat.

TATER TOT TACO CASSEROLE
Servings: 8 | Prep: 15m | Cooks: 1h | Total: 1h15m

NUTRITION FACTS

Calories: 477 | Carbohydrates: 38.4g | Fat: 27g | Protein: 24.9g | Cholesterol: 76mg

INGREDIENTS

- 1 pound ground beef
- 1 (12 ounce) can black beans, rinsed and drained
- 1 small onion, diced
- 1 (12 ounce) bag shredded Mexican cheese blend
- 1 clove garlic, minced
- 1 (16 ounce) package frozen tater tots

- 1 (1 ounce) packet taco seasoning mix
- 1 (12 fluid ounce) can enchilada sauce
- 1 (16 ounce) bag frozen Mexican-style corn

DIRECTIONS

1. Preheat an oven to 375 degrees F (190 degrees C). Prepare a 9x13-inch baking dish with cooking spray.
2. Cook the ground beef in a skillet over medium heat until completely browned, 5 to 7 minutes. Add the onion, garlic, taco seasoning mix, frozen Mexican-style corn, and black beans to the ground beef; cook and stir another 10 minutes. Set aside to cool slightly.
3. Combine the ground beef mixture in a large bowl with about 3/4 of the Mexican cheese blend and the tater tots; stir to combine.
4. Pour about 1/3 of the enchilada sauce into the bottom of the prepared baking dish. Add the tater tot mixture to the baking dish; lightly pat the mixture down into a solid, even layer. Pour the remaining enchilada sauce over the tater tot layer.
5. Bake in the preheated oven for 40 minutes. Sprinkle the remaining Mexican cheese over the casserole and return to oven until the cheese is melted and bubbly, about 5 minutes more.

LIME CILANTRO RICE

Servings: 4 | Prep: 10m | Cooks: 20m | Total: 30m

NUTRITION FACTS

Calories: 84 | Carbohydrates: 12.7g | Fat: 3.1g | Protein: 2.4g | Cholesterol: 8mg

INGREDIENTS

- 2 cups water
- 1 teaspoon lime zest
- 1 tablespoon butter
- 2 tablespoons fresh lime juice
- 1 cup long-grain white rice
- 1/2 cup chopped cilantro

DIRECTIONS

1. Bring the water to a boil; stir the butter and rice into the water. Cover, reduce heat to low, and simmer until the rice is tender, about 20 minutes.
2. Stir the lime zest, lime juice, and cilantro into the cooked rice just before serving.

CHURROS

Servings: 4 | Prep: 10m | Cooks: 10m | Total: 20m

NUTRITION FACTS

Calories: 691 | Carbohydrates: 57.1g | Fat: g | Protein: 3.3g | Cholesterol: 0mg

INGREDIENTS

- 1 cup water
- 1 cup all-purpose flour
- 2 1/2 tablespoons white sugar
- 2 quarts oil for frying
- 1/2 teaspoon salt
- 1/2 cup white sugar, or to taste
- 2 tablespoons vegetable oil
- 1 teaspoon ground cinnamon

DIRECTIONS

1. In a small saucepan over medium heat, combine water, 2 1/2 tablespoons sugar, salt and 2 tablespoons vegetable oil. Bring to a boil and remove from heat. Stir in flour until mixture forms a ball.
2. Heat oil for frying in deep-fryer or deep skillet to 375 degrees F (190 degrees C). Pipe strips of dough into hot oil using a pastry bag. Fry until golden; drain on paper towels.
3. Combine 1/2 cup sugar and cinnamon. Roll drained churros in cinnamon and sugar mixture.

VEGETARIAN TORTILLA SOUP
Servings: 12 | Prep: 15m | Cooks: 40m | Total: 55m

NUTRITION FACTS

Calories: 315 | Carbohydrates: 37.2g | Fat: 16.2g | Protein: 8.7g | Cholesterol: 12mg

INGREDIENTS

- 2 tablespoons vegetable oil
- 4 (14 ounce) cans vegetable broth
- 1 (1 pound) package frozen pepper and onion stir fry mix
- salt and pepper to taste
- 2 cloves garlic, minced
- 1 (11 ounce) can whole kernel corn
- 3 tablespoons ground cumin
- 12 ounces tortilla chips
- 1 (28 ounce) can crushed tomatoes
- 1 cup shredded Cheddar cheese
- 3 (4 ounce) cans chopped green chile peppers, drained
- 1 avocado - peeled, pitted and diced

DIRECTIONS

1. Heat the oil in a large pot over medium heat. Stir in the pepper and onion stir fry mix, garlic, and cumin, and cook 5 minutes, until vegetables are tender. Mix in the tomatoes and chile peppers. Pour in the broth, and season with salt and pepper. Bring to a boil, reduce heat to low, and simmer 30 minutes.
2. Mix corn into the soup, and continue cooking 5 minutes. Serve in bowls over equal amounts of tortilla chips. Top with cheese and avocado.

SWEET CORN CAKE
Servings: 6 | Prep: 15m | Cooks: 1h | Total: 1h15m

NUTRITION FACTS

Calories: 273 | Carbohydrates: 27.9g | Fat: 18.1g | Protein: 2.6g | Cholesterol: 47mg

INGREDIENTS

- 1/2 cup butter, softened
- 1/3 cup white sugar
- 1/3 cup masa harina
- 2 tablespoons heavy whipping cream
- 1/4 cup water
- 1/4 teaspoon salt
- 1 1/2 cups frozen whole-kernel corn, thawed
- 1/2 teaspoon baking powder
- 1/4 cup cornmeal

DIRECTIONS

1. In a medium bowl beat butter until it is creamy. Add the Mexican corn flour and water and beat until well mixed.
2. Using a food processor, process thawed corn, but leave chunky. Stir into the butter mixture.
3. In a separate bowl, mix cornmeal, sugar, cream, salt, and baking powder. Add to corn flour mixture and stir to combine. Pour batter into an ungreased 8x8 inch baking pan. Smooth batter and cover with aluminum foil. Place pan into a 9x13 inch baking dish that is filled a third of the way with water.
4. Bake in a preheated 350 degree oven F (175 degrees C) oven for 50 to 60 minutes. Allow to cool for 10 minutes. Use an ice cream scoop for easy removal from pan.

CHICKEN ENCHILADA CASSEROLE
Servings: 12 | Prep: 30m | Cooks: 30m | Total: 1h

NUTRITION FACTS

Calories: 537 | Carbohydrates: 39.9g | Fat: 28.1g | Protein: 31.4g | Cholesterol: 95mg

INGREDIENTS

- 1 (16 ounce) container sour cream
- 1 (8 ounce) can chili beans, drained
- 1 (16 ounce) jar salsa
- 6 (12 inch) flour tortillas, cut into strips
- 1 (10.75 ounce) can condensed cream of chicken soup
- 6 skinless, boneless chicken breast halves - cooked and shredded
- ¼ cup diced onion
- 4 cups shredded Cheddar cheese

DIRECTIONS

1. Preheat oven to 350 degrees F (175 degrees C).
2. In a large bowl, mix sour cream, salsa, cream of chicken soup, onion and chili beans.
3. Layer the bottom of a 9x13 inch baking dish with 1/3 tortilla strips. Top with 1/3 chicken, 1/3 sour cream mixture and 1/3 Cheddar cheese. Repeat layering with remaining ingredients.
4. Bake in the preheated oven 20 to 30 minutes, or until golden and bubbly. Let stand about 10 minutes, or as long as you can stand it!!! You're done.

SOPAPILLA CHEESECAKE DESSERT
Servings: 12 | Prep: 15m | Cooks: 45m | Total: 3h | Additional: 2h

NUTRITION FACTS

Calories: 553 | Carbohydrates: 50.1g | Fat: 36.2g | Protein: 7.4g | Cholesterol: 82mg

INGREDIENTS

- 3 (8 ounce) packages cream cheese, softened
- 1/2 cup melted butter
- 11/2 cups white sugar
- 1/2 cup white sugar
- 1 1/2 teaspoons vanilla extract
- 1 teaspoon ground cinnamon
- 2 (8 ounce) cans crescent roll dough
- 1/4 cup sliced almonds

DIRECTIONS

1. Preheat an oven to 350 degrees F (175 degrees C).

2. Beat the cream cheese with 1 1/2 cups of sugar, and the vanilla extract in a bowl until smooth. Unroll the cans of crescent roll dough, and use a rolling pin to shape the each piece into 9x13 inch rectangles. Press one piece into the bottom of a 9x13 inch baking dish. Evenly spread the cream cheese mixture into the baking dish, then cover with the remaining piece of crescent dough.

3. Drizzle the melted butter evenly over the top of the cheesecake. Stir the remaining 1/2 cup of sugar together with the cinnamon in a small bowl, and sprinkle over the cheesecake along with the almonds.

4. Bake in the preheated oven until the crescent dough has puffed and turned golden brown, about 45 minutes. Cool completely in the pan before cutting into 12 squares.

ENCHILADAS SUIZAS
Servings: 6 | Prep: 45m | Cooks: 20m | Total: 1h5m

NUTRITION FACTS

Calories: 7.3 | Carbohydrates: 42.3g | Fat: 52.1g | Protein: 28.5g | Cholesterol: 136mg

INGREDIENTS

- 2 tablespoons butter
- canola oil for frying
- 2/3 cup chopped Spanish onion
- 1 cup shredded Monterey Jack cheese
- 2 tablespoons all-purpose flour
- 1 cup shredded mild Cheddar cheese
- 1 1/2 cups chicken broth
- 2 cups shredded, cooked chicken breast meat
- 1 cup chopped green chile peppers
- 1 cup heavy cream
- 1 clove garlic, minced
- 1/4 cup chopped green onion
- 3/4 teaspoon salt
- 1/2 cup sliced green olives
- 1 dash ground cumin
- 1 pint cherry tomatoes
- 12 (8 inch) corn tortillas

DIRECTIONS

1. Prepare salsa verde: Melt butter in saucepan over medium heat. Saute the onion until soft. Stir in the flour. Add the broth, then add the chiles, garlic, salt, and cumin. Simmer about 15 minutes to blend flavors, then set aside. Preheat oven to 350 degrees F (175 degrees C.)

2. In a heavy skillet, lightly fry tortillas in shallow oil, being careful not to make them too crisp to roll. Combine the cheeses and keep 1/2 cup aside for topping. Dip each tortilla in salsa verde (both sides.) Place 2 heaping tablespoons chicken and about 2 tablespoons cheese down the center of each; roll and place seam side down in a shallow dish.

3. After all the rolled tortillas are in the dish, spoon additional salsa verde over them and then cover evenly with heavy cream. Sprinkle with remaining 1/2 cup cheese mixture, and with the green onions.

4. Bake uncovered in preheated oven for 20 minutes. Serve immediately, garnished with the olives, cherry tomatoes, and with additional salsa on the side.

MEXICAN CHICKEN CORN CHOWDER
Servings: 8 | Prep: 20m | Cooks: 35m | Total: 55m

NUTRITION FACTS

Calories: 367 | Carbohydrates: 15.1g | Fat: 21.3g | Protein: 30g | Cholesterol: 109mg

INGREDIENTS

- 1 1/2 pounds boneless skinless chicken breasts, cut into bite-size pieces
- 2 cups half-and-half cream
- 1/2 cup chopped onion
- 2 cups shredded Monterey Jack cheese
- 1 clove garlic, minced
- 1 (14.75 ounce) can cream-style corn
- 3 tablespoons butter
- 1 (4 ounce) can diced green chiles
- 2 cubes chicken bouillon
- 1 dash hot pepper sauce
- 1 cup hot water
- 1 tomato, chopped
- 3/4 teaspoon ground cumin
- fresh cilantro sprigs, for garnish (optional)

DIRECTIONS

1. In a Dutch oven, brown chicken, onion, and garlic in butter until chicken is no longer pink.
2. Dissolve the bouillon in hot water; Pour into Dutch oven, and season with cumin. Bring to a boil. Reduce heat to low, cover, and simmer for 5 minutes.
3. Stir in cream, cheese, corn, chilies, and hot pepper sauce. Cook, stirring frequently, until the cheese is melted. Stir in chopped tomato. Garnish with cilantro.

CHICKEN FIESTA SALAD

Servings: 4 | Prep: 10m | Cooks: 30m | Total: 40m

NUTRITION FACTS

Calories: 311 | Carbohydrates: 42.2g | Fat: 6.4g | Protein: 23g | Cholesterol: 36mg

INGREDIENTS

- 2 skinless, boneless chicken breast halves
- 1/2 cup salsa
- 1 (1.27 ounce) packet dry fajita seasoning, divided
- 1 (10 ounce) package mixed salad greens
- 1 tablespoon vegetable oil
- 1 onion, chopped
- 1 (15 ounce) can black beans, rinsed and drained
- 1 tomato, cut into wedges
- 1 (11 ounce) can Mexican-style corn

DIRECTIONS

1. Rub chicken evenly with 1/2 the fajita seasoning. Heat the oil in a skillet over medium heat, and cook the chicken 8 minutes on each side, or until juices run clear; set aside.
2. In a large saucepan, mix beans, corn, salsa and other 1/2 of fajita seasoning. Heat over medium heat until warm.
3. Prepare the salad by tossing the greens, onion and tomato. Top salad with chicken and dress with the bean and corn mixture.

WHIT'S CHICKEN ENCHILADAS

Servings: 8 | Prep: 30m | Cooks: 30m | Total: 1h

NUTRITION FACTS

Calories: 706 | Carbohydrates: 38.7g | Fat: 44g | Protein: 38.1g | Cholesterol: 160mg

INGREDIENTS

- 4 bone-in chicken breast halves
- 1 (8 ounce) package cream cheese
- 2 tablespoons olive oil
- 2 cups shredded Monterey Jack cheese, divided
- 1 (4 ounce) can diced green chile peppers, drained
- 1/2 cup water
- 1 jalapeno pepper, chopped

- 8 (10 inch) flour tortillas
- 1 clove garlic, minced
- 1 cup heavy cream

DIRECTIONS

1. Place the chicken breast halves into a saucepan, and fill with enough water to cover. Bring to a boil, and cook until the chicken is cooked through, about 20 minutes. Remove from the water, and set aside to cool.
2. Preheat the oven to 375 degrees F (190 degrees C). Remove the chicken meat from the breasts, and discard the skin and bones. Set aside.
3. Heat the olive oil in a large skillet over medium heat. Add the green chilies, jalapeno and garlic. Cook and stir for a few minutes, until fragrant, then stir in the cream cheese and half of the Monterey Jack. As the cheese begins to melt, gradually stir in the water. Chop the chicken meat, and stir into the skillet. Remove from the heat.
4. Spoon the chicken mixture into tortillas, and roll up. Place the rolls seam side down in a 9x13 inch baking dish. Sprinkle the remaining Monterey Jack cheese over the top, then pour cream over all.

MAKE AHEAD LUNCH WRAPS
Servings: 16 | Prep: 30m | Cooks: 35m | Total: 1h5m

NUTRITION FACTS

Calories: 557 | Carbohydrates: 80.8g | Fat: 16g | Protein: 22.9g | Cholesterol: 30mg

INGREDIENTS

- 2 cups uncooked brown rice
- 1 (10 ounce) can whole kernel corn
- 4 cups water
- 1 (10 ounce) can diced tomatoes and green chiles
- 4 (15 ounce) cans black beans
- 16 (10 inch) flour tortillas
- 2 (15.5 ounce) cans pinto beans
- 1 pound shredded pepperjack cheese

DIRECTIONS

1. Combine rice and water in a saucepan, and bring to a boil. Reduce heat to low, cover, and simmer for 35 to 40 minutes, or until tender. Remove from heat, and cool.
2. Place black beans and pinto beans into a colander or strainer, and rinse. Add corn and diced tomatoes with green chilies, and toss to mix. Transfer to a large bowl, and mix in rice and cheese.
3. Divide the mixture evenly among the tortillas, and roll up. Wrap individually in plastic wrap, place into a large freezer bag, and freeze. Reheat as needed in the microwave for lunch or snacks.

HOT BEAN DIP

Servings: 20 | Prep: 10m | Cooks: 30m | Total: 40m

NUTRITION FACTS

Calories: 196 | Carbohydrates: 8.6g | Fat: 14g | Protein: 9.3g | Cholesterol: 43mg

INGREDIENTS

- 1 (8 ounce) package cream cheese, softened
- 2 tablespoons dried parsley
- 1 cup sour cream
- 1/4 cup chopped green onions
- 2 (16 ounce) cans refried beans
- 1 (8 ounce) package shredded Cheddar cheese
- 1/2 (1 ounce) package taco seasoning mix
- 1 (8 ounce) package shredded Monterey Jack cheese
- 5 drops hot pepper sauce

DIRECTIONS

1. Preheat oven to 350 degrees F (175 degrees C).
2. In a medium bowl, blend the cream cheese and sour cream. Mix in the refried beans, taco seasoning, hot pepper sauce, parsley, green onions, 1/2 the Cheddar cheese and 1/2 the Monterey Jack cheese. Transfer the mixture to an 8x12 inch baking dish. Top with remaining Cheddar and Monterey Jack cheeses.
3. Bake in the preheated oven 20 to 30 minutes, until cheese is slightly browned.

NACHO CHEESE SAUCE

Servings: 4 | Prep: 10m | Cooks: 15m | Total: 25m

NUTRITION FACTS

Calories: 282 | Carbohydrates: 6.6g | Fat: 22.5g | Protein: 13.5g | Cholesterol: 67mg

INGREDIENTS

- 2 tablespoons butter
- 7 slices processed American cheese
- 2 tablespoons all-purpose flour
- 1/2 teaspoon salt
- 1 cup milk

DIRECTIONS

1. In a medium saucepan over medium heat, melt butter and stir in flour. Pour in the milk and stir until the mixture thickens. Stirring constantly, mix in cheese and salt. Continue to cook and stir until cheese has melted and all ingredients are well blended, about 15 minutes

SOUR CREAM CHICKEN ENCHILADAS
Servings: 12 | Prep: 20m | Cooks: 30m | Total: 50m

NUTRITION FACTS

Calories: 265 | Carbohydrates: 22.8g | Fat: 13.3g | Protein: 13.1g | Cholesterol: 40mg

INGREDIENTS

- 1 bunch cilantro
- 2 skinless, boneless chicken breast halves, cooked and shredded
- 1 cup sour cream
- 1 onion
- 2 (7 ounce) cans jalapeno salsa
- 12 (6 inch) flour tortillas
- 2 (7 ounce) cans prepared green chile salsa
- 2 cups shredded Cheddar cheese

DIRECTIONS

1. To Make Sour Cream Mixture: In a blender or food processor, puree cilantro, sour cream, jalapeno salsa and 1/2 can of the green chile salsa. Set aside.
2. To Make Chicken Mixture: In a large bowl, combine shredded chicken, onion and the remaining 1 1/2 cans of green chile salsa. Mix well.
3. Preheat oven to 350 degrees F (175 degrees C).
4. Heat tortillas in conventional or microwave oven until soft. Pour enough of the sour cream mixture into a 9x13 inch baking dish to coat the bottom. Place 2 heaping tablespoonfuls of the chicken mixture in each tortilla, roll up and place seam side down in the baking dish. Pour remaining sour cream mixture over all and top with shredded cheese.
5. Cover dish tightly with aluminum foil and bake at 350 degrees F (175 degrees C) for about 30 minutes, or until dish is heated through and bubbling.

CHICKEN CHIMICHANGAS WITH SOUR CREAM SAUCE
Servings: 8 | Prep: 25m | Cooks: 40m | Total: 1h5m

NUTRITION FACTS

Calories: 506 | Carbohydrates: 33.3g | Fat: 30g | Protein: 25.7g | Cholesterol: 72mg

INGREDIENTS

- 2 large skinless, boneless chicken breast halves
- 3 large cloves garlic, minced
- 3 cups water
- 2 tablespoons butter
- 1 tablespoon chili powder
- 2 tablespoons all-purpose flour
- 1/2 teaspoon salt
- 1 cup water
- 1/2 teaspoon ground cumin
- 1 cube chicken bouillon
- 1/4 teaspoon ground black pepper
- 1/2 cup sour cream
- 1/4 teaspoon garlic powder
- salt and pepper to taste
- 1/4 teaspoon onion powder
- oil for frying
- 1/8 teaspoon cayenne pepper
- 8 (8 inch) flour tortillas
- 1 (7 ounce) can chopped green chilies, divided
- 8 ounces shredded Monterey Jack cheese
- 1/2 cup diced onion

DIRECTIONS

1. Place the chicken breasts into a large saucepan. Pour in the water, and season with chili powder, 1/2 teaspoon salt, cumin, 1/4 teaspoon black pepper, garlic powder, onion powder, and cayenne pepper. Bring to a simmer over high heat, then reduce heat to medium-low, and simmer 15 minutes. After 15 minutes, stir in 4 ounces of green chiles, onion, and garlic; continue simmering until the liquid has reduced to 1 cup. Reserve remaining 3 ounces of chopped green chilies. Remove the chicken, shred with two forks, and return to the onion mixture.
2. Meanwhile, melt the butter in a small saucepan over medium heat. Stir in the flour, and cook for 1 minute. Whisk in the water and bouillon cube until the water has thickened and the bouillon cube has dissolved, about 4 minutes. Whisk in reserved 3 ounces of green chilies and the sour cream; season to taste with salt and pepper. Keep warm.
3. Heat oil in a deep-fryer or large saucepan to 375 degrees F (190 degrees C
4. Place a tortilla onto your work surface, then spoon about 1/3 cup of the chicken filling halfway between the bottom edge and the center of the tortilla. Flatten the filling into rectangle shape with the back of a spoon. Sprinkle about 1 ounce of the Monterey Jack cheese over the filling. Fold the bottom of the tortilla snugly over the filling, then fold in the left and right edges. Roll the chimichanga up to the top edge, forming a tight cylinder; secure the ends with wooden toothpicks. Repeat with the remaining ingredients.

5. Cook the chimichangas, 2 at a time, in the hot oil until they are crisp and golden brown on both sides, about 1 minute per side. Drain on a paper towel-lined plate, and remove toothpicks. Top with sour cream sauce to serve.

ALBONDIGAS

Servings: 6 | Prep: 20m | Cooks: 20m | Total: 40m

NUTRITION FACTS

Calories: 325 | Carbohydrates: 20.4g | Fat: 17.1g | Protein: 22.6g | Cholesterol: 72mg

INGREDIENTS

- 1 quart water
- 2 beef bouillon cubes
- 4 carrots, sliced
- 1 1/2 pounds ground beef
- 2 small potatoes, peeled and diced
- 1/3 cup seasoned dry bread crumbs
- 1 medium onion, diced
- 1/3 cup milk
- 1 1/2 cups salsa, medium or hot
- chopped fresh cilantro (optional)

DIRECTIONS

1. In a large stock pot, bring water, carrots, potatoes, onion, salsa, and bouillon cubes to a boil. Reduce to a medium simmer, stirring occasionally, approximately 10 minutes.
2. Mix the beef, breadcrumbs, and milk together in a bowl. Form into 1-inch meatballs, and drop into boiling broth. Once soup returns to a boil, reduce heat to medium-low.
3. Cover and cook 20 minutes, or until meatballs are no longer pink in center and vegetables are tender. Serve with sprinkled cilantro for garnish.

JIMMY'S MEXICAN PIZZA

Servings: 8 | Prep: 20m | Cooks: 25m | Total: 45m

NUTRITION FACTS

Calories: 370 | Carbohydrates: 31.6g | Fat: 18.6g | Protein: 19.6g | Cholesterol: 55mg

INGREDIENTS

- 1/2 pound ground beef
- 4 (10 inch) flour tortillas

- 1 medium onion, diced
- 1/2 cup salsa
- 1 clove garlic, minced
- 1 cup shredded Cheddar cheese
- 1 tablespoon chili powder
- 1 cup shredded Monterey Jack cheese
- 1 teaspoon ground cumin
- 2 green onions, chopped
- 1/2 teaspoon paprika
- 2 roma (plum) tomatoes, diced
- 1/2 teaspoon black pepper
- 1/4 cup thinly sliced jalapeno pepper
- 1/2 teaspoon salt
- 1/4 cup sour cream (optional)
- 1 (16 ounce) can refried beans

DIRECTIONS

1. Preheat the oven to 350 degrees F (175 degrees C). Coat 2 pie plates with non-stick cooking spray.
2. Place beef, onion and garlic in a skillet over medium heat. Cook until beef is evenly browned. Drain off grease. Season the meat with chili powder, cumin, paprika, salt and pepper.
3. Lay one tortilla in each pie plate, and cover with a layer of refried beans. Spread half of the seasoned ground beef over each one, and then cover with a second tortilla. Bake for 10 minutes in the preheated oven.
4. Remove the plates from the oven, and let cool slightly. Spread half of the salsa over each top tortilla. Cover each pizza with half of the Cheddar and Monterey Jack cheeses. Place half of the tomatoes, half of the green onions, and half of the jalapeno slices onto each one.
5. Return the pizzas to the oven, and bake for 5 to 10 more minutes, until the cheese is melted. Remove from the oven, and let cool slightly before slicing each one into 4 pieces.

SEVEN LAYER DIP

Servings: 15 | Prep: 15m | Cooks: 0m | Total: 15m

NUTRITION FACTS

Calories: 277 | Carbohydrates: 9.3g | Fat: 19.5g | Protein: 16.8g | Cholesterol: 63mg

INGREDIENTS

- 1 1/2 pounds ground beef
- 1 cup salsa
- 1 (16 ounce) can refried beans
- 1 (2.25 ounce) can black olives, chopped
- 4 cups shredded Cheddar-Monterey Jack cheese blend

- 1/2 cup chopped tomatoes
- 1 (8 ounce) container sour cream
- 1/2 cup chopped green onions
- 1 cup guacamole

DIRECTIONS

1. In a large skillet, brown ground beef. Set aside to drain and cool to room temperature.
2. Spread the beans into the bottom of a 9x13 inch serving tray that is about 1 1/2 inches deep. Sprinkle 2 cups of shredded cheese on top of beans. Sprinkle beef on top of cheese. Spread sour cream very slowly on top of beef. Spread guacamole on top of sour cream. Pour salsa over guacamole and spread evenly. Sprinkle remaining shredded cheese. Sprinkle black olives, tomatoes, and green onions on top.
3. You can serve this dish immediately, or refrigerate it over night and serve cold. I think it tastes better at room temperature.

AUTHENTIC ENCHILADAS VERDES

Servings: 4 | Prep: 45m | Cooks: 35m | Total: 1h20m

NUTRITION FACTS

Calories: 559 | Carbohydrates: 48.9g | Fat: 25g | Protein: 37.1g | Cholesterol: 84mg

INGREDIENTS

- 2 bone-in chicken breast halves
- 1 clove garlic
- 2 cups chicken broth
- 1 pinch salt
- 1/4 white onion
- 12 corn tortillas
- 1 clove garlic
- 1/4 cup vegetable oil
- 2 teaspoons salt
- 1 cup crumbled queso fresco
- 1 pound fresh tomatillos, husks removed
- 1/2 white onion, chopped
- 5 serrano peppers
- 1 bunch fresh cilantro, chopped
- 1/4 white onion

DIRECTIONS

1. In a saucepan, combine chicken breast with chicken broth, one quarter onion, a clove of garlic, and 2 teaspoons salt. Bring to a boil, and then boil for 20 minutes. Reserve broth, set chicken aside to cool, and discard onion and garlic. When cool enough to handle, shred chicken with your hands.
2. Place tomatillos and serrano chiles in a pot with water, enough to cover them. Bring to boil, and continue boiling until tomatillos turn a different shade of green (from bright green to a dull, army green). Strain tomatillos and chiles, and place in a blender with another quarter piece of onion, 1 clove garlic, and a pinch of salt. Pour in reserved chicken broth, so that liquid just covers the veggies in the blender by about an inch. Blend all ingredients until they are completely pureed. Pour salsa in a medium saucepan, and bring to a low boil.
3. Pour oil in a frying pan, and allow to get very hot. Slightly fry tortillas one by one in hot oil, setting each on a paper towel afterwards to soak some of the oil. Finally, dip slightly fried tortillas in low-boiling green salsa, until tortillas become soft again. Place on plates, 3 per person.
4. Fill or top tortillas with shredded chicken, then extra green sauce. Top with crumbled cheese, chopped onion, and chopped cilantro.

GERRY'S CHICKEN ENCHILADAS

Servings: 6 | Prep: 30m | Cooks: 55m | Total: 1h55m

NUTRITION FACTS

Calories: 718 | Carbohydrates: 38.1g | Fat: 46.8g | Protein: 40.2g | Cholesterol: 182mg

INGREDIENTS

- 4 boneless, skinless chicken breast halves
- 1 (14.5 ounce) can chicken broth
- 1 tablespoon vegetable oil
- 1 bunch green onions, chopped
- 1 onion, chopped
- 1/2 pint heavy cream
- 1 (10 ounce) can diced tomatoes with green chile peppers
- 6 (6 inch) corn tortillas
- 1 (14.5 ounce) can stewed tomatoes
- 3 cups shredded Cheddar cheese
- 12 small chile peppers, diced (optional)
- 1 (10 ounce) can enchilada sauce
- 1 (10.75 ounce) can condensed cream of chicken soup

DIRECTIONS

1. Cut chicken breasts into 1 inch strips. Place in a medium bowl with desired marinade, and marinate in the refrigerator for at least 30 minutes.
2. Preheat oven to 350 degrees F (175 degrees C).

3. Heat oil in a large skillet over medium heat. Saute chicken and onions until chicken is evenly brown. Stir in diced tomatoes with green chile peppers, stewed tomatoes, chile peppers, soup and broth. Bring mixture to a boil. Reduce heat, cover skillet, and simmer for 20 to 30 minutes, or until chicken is no longer pink and juices run clear.
4. Remove chicken from skillet, and shred when cool enough to handle. Meanwhile, allow skillet mixture to simmer and reduce to about 2 1/4 cups. In a medium bowl, combine shredded chicken and about 1/4 cup skillet mixture (just enough to make a paste like mixture). Mix together with half the chopped green onions. Pour remaining 2 cups of skillet mixture into a 9x13 inch baking dish.
5. In a second skillet, heat cream over low heat, being careful not to boil. Dip tortillas in the warm cream to soften and coat. Spoon about 1/3 cup chicken mixture onto each tortilla. Top chicken mixture with half the shredded cheese, and roll up tortillas. Place rolled tortillas in baking dish, seam side down, and drizzle with enchilada sauce. Cover with remaining shredded cheese, and sprinkle remaining chopped green onion over cheese. Bake uncovered in preheated oven for 25 minutes, or until cheese is melted and bubbling.

RESTAURANT STYLE CHICKEN NACHOS
Servings: 6 | Prep: 30m | Cooks: 10m | Total: 40m

NUTRITION FACTS

Calories: 407 | Carbohydrates: 24.4g | Fat: 25.7g | Protein: 21.4g | Cholesterol: 54mg

INGREDIENTS

- 2 cloves garlic, crushed
- 1 cup salsa
- 6 green onions, sliced, white parts and tops separated
- 1/2 (12 ounce) package tortilla chips
- 3 tablespoons canola oil
- 1 (8 ounce) package shredded Cheddar/Monterey Jack cheese blend
- 1 shredded, cooked, whole chicken breast
- 1/2 large tomato, diced
- salt and pepper to taste

DIRECTIONS

1. Preheat oven to 350 degrees F (175 degrees C).
2. In a 12 inch skillet over medium heat, cook and stir the garlic and white parts of the green onions in canola oil until tender. Mix in shredded chicken, salt and pepper. Toss until well coated with oil. Stir in the salsa.
3. Arrange tortilla chips on a large baking sheet. Spoon the chicken mixture over tortilla chips. Top with Cheddar/Monterey Jack cheese blend and tomato. Bake in the preheated oven 10 minutes, or until cheese has melted. Remove from heat and sprinkle with green onion tops before serving.

MEXICAN LASAGNA

Servings: 5 | Prep: 25m | Cooks: 20m | Total: 45m

NUTRITION FACTS

Calories: 447 | Carbohydrates: 33.2g | Fat: 24g | Protein: 23.2g | Cholesterol: 79mg

INGREDIENTS

- 1 pound lean ground beef
- 10 (6 inch) corn tortillas
- 1 (1 ounce) package taco seasoning mix
- 1 cup prepared salsa
- 1 (14 ounce) can peeled and diced tomatoes with juice
- 1/2 cup shredded Colby cheese

DIRECTIONS

1. Preheat oven to 350 degrees F (175 degrees C).
2. In a large skillet over medium-high heat, brown the ground beef, and stir in the taco seasoning and tomatoes. Line a 9x13-inch baking dish with half the tortillas. Spoon the beef mixture into the dish, then top with the remaining tortillas. Spread salsa over the tortillas and sprinkle with the cheese.
3. Bake at 350 degrees F (175 degrees C) for 20 to 30 minutes, or until cheese is melted and bubbly.

TOMATILLO SALSA VERDE

Servings: 8 | Prep: 10m | Cooks: 15m | Total: m

NUTRITION FACTS

Calories: 24 | Carbohydrates: 4.6g | Fat: 0.6g | Protein: 0.8g | Cholesterol: 0mg

INGREDIENTS

- 1 pound tomatillos, husked
- 1 tablespoon chopped fresh oregano
- 1/2 cup finely chopped onion
- 1/2 teaspoon ground cumin
- 1 teaspoon minced garlic
- 1 1/2 teaspoons salt, or to taste
- 1 serrano chile peppers, minced
- 2 cups water
- 2 tablespoons chopped cilantro

DIRECTIONS

1. Place tomatillos, onion, garlic, and chile pepper into a saucepan. Season with cilantro, oregano, cumin, and salt; pour in water. Bring to a boil over high heat, then reduce heat to medium-low, and simmer until the tomatillos are soft, 10 to 15 minutes.
2. Using a blender, carefully puree the tomatillos and water in batches until smooth.

CILANTRO-LIME DRESSING

Servings: 16 | Prep: 30m | Cooks: 0m | Total: 30m

NUTRITION FACTS

Calories: 87 | Carbohydrates: 6.4g | Fat: 7g | Protein: 0.1g | Cholesterol: 0mg

INGREDIENTS

- 1 jalapeno pepper, seeded and coarsely chopped
- 2 teaspoons balsamic vinegar
- 1 clove garlic
- 1/2 teaspoon salt, or to taste
- 3/4 teaspoon minced fresh ginger root
- 1/4 cup packed cilantro leaves
- 1/4 cup lime juice
- 1/2 cup extra-virgin olive oil
- 1/3 cup honey

DIRECTIONS

1. Place the jalapeno pepper, garlic clove, and ginger into a food processor or blender; pulse until the jalapeno and garlic are finely chopped. Pour in the lime juice, honey, balsamic vinegar, and salt, add the cilantro leaves; pulse a few times to blend. Turn the food processor or blender on, and slowly drizzle in the olive oil until incorporated into the dressing. Season to taste with salt before serving.

HOT TAMALE PIE

Servings: 8 | Prep: 20m | Cooks: 1h10m | Total: 1h30m

NUTRITION FACTS

Calories: 640 | Carbohydrates: 54.3g | Fat: 31.8g | Protein: 34.4g | Cholesterol: 146mg

INGREDIENTS

- cooking spray
- 2 (8.5 ounce) boxes dry corn muffin mix (such as Jiffy)
- 2 pounds ground beef
- 2 eggs

- 2 cups diced poblano peppers
- 2/3 cup milk, divided
- 1 teaspoon salt
- 4 ounces shredded Cheddar cheese, divided
- 1 (16 ounce) jar salsa
- 4 ounces shredded Monterey Jack cheese, divided
- 1/2 teaspoon dried oregano
- 8 ounces frozen corn, thawed
- 1 teaspoon ground dried chipotle pepper

DIRECTIONS

1. Preheat the oven to 350 degrees F (175 degrees C).
2. Spray a 9x13-inch casserole dish with cooking spray.
3. Cook and stir ground beef in a Dutch oven over medium-high heat until meat starts to brown and release juices, about 5 minutes.
4. Reduce heat to medium and stir in poblano peppers, salt, salsa, oregano, and chipotle powder; cook and stir until seasoned beef is crumbly and no longer pink, about 10 minutes.
5. Mix one package of corn muffin mix in a large bowl with 1 egg and 1/3 cup of milk. Whisk to combine. In a separate large bowl, mix the second package of corn muffin mix with 1 egg, 1/3 cup of milk and half the Cheddar and Monterey Jack cheeses.
6. Spread the prepared corn muffin mixture without cheese into the prepared baking dish. Sprinkle corn over the muffin mix, followed by remaining half of the cheeses, then the beef mixture.
7. Spoon the corn muffin mix with cheese on top of the beef and carefully spread over the top with a fork, leaving about half an inch from the edges of the pan.
8. Bake in the preheated oven for 50-60 minutes, until golden brown.

MEXICAN BEEF CASSEROLE
Servings: 12 | Prep: 30m | Cooks: 30m | Total: 1h

NUTRITION FACTS

Calories: 383 | Carbohydrates: 21.8g | Fat: 22.9g | Protein: 22.4g | Cholesterol: 71mg

INGREDIENTS

- 1 pound lean ground beef
- 1 (12 ounce) package corn tortillas
- 1 (15 ounce) can ranch-style beans
- 4 cups shredded Cheddar cheese
- 1 (14.5 ounce) can peeled and diced tomatoes
- 2 tablespoons chili powder
- 1 (10.75 ounce) can condensed cream of mushroom soup

DIRECTIONS

1. Preheat oven to 350 degrees F (175 degrees C).
2. Brown the ground beef in a large skillet over medium high heat. Add chili powder, beans, tomatoes and soup; mix well and heat thoroughly.
3. Line a 13x9 inch dish with tortillas. Then make a layer with the meat mixture. Make another row of tortillas, then finish off with rest of meat mixture. Top with grated cheese.
4. Bake in a preheated oven for 30 minutes.

TACO LASAGNA

Servings: 12 | Prep: 20m | Cooks: 45m | Total: 1h15m

NUTRITION FACTS

Calories: 475 | Carbohydrates: 28.2g | Fat: 28.5g | Protein: 26.7g | Cholesterol: 97mg

INGREDIENTS

- 2 pounds lean ground beef
- 18 (6 inch) corn tortillas
- 2 (1.25 ounce) packages taco seasoning mix
- 1 (24 ounce) jar salsa
- 4 cloves garlic, minced
- 1 cup sliced green onion
- 1/2 teaspoon cayenne pepper
- 1 (16 ounce) container sour cream
- 1 tablespoon chili powder
- 1 1/2 cups shredded Cheddar cheese
- 1/2 cup water
- 1 1/2 cups shredded Monterey Jack cheese

DIRECTIONS

1. Place ground beef in a large, deep skillet. Cook over medium high heat until evenly brown. Drain, then season with taco seasoning, garlic, cayenne pepper, chili powder and water. Simmer for 10 minutes.
2. Preheat oven to 375 degrees F (190 degrees C). Grease the bottom of a 9x13 inch baking dish.
3. Place 6 tortillas into the prepared baking dish. Spread 1/3 of the salsa on top of the tortillas. Spread 1/2 of the meat mixture evenly over the salsa. Sprinkle with 1/2 of the green onions. Drop 1/2 of the sour cream randomly over the green onions. Top with 1/2 cup Cheddar and 1/2 cup Monterey Jack cheese. Repeat layers. Top with 6 tortillas, spread with remaining salsa, and sprinkle with remaining cheese.
4. Bake in a preheated oven for 30 to 45 minutes or until cheeses are melted.

LISA'S FAVORITE CARNE ASADA MARINADE

Servings: 12 | Prep: 20m | Cooks: 10m | Total: 1d40m

NUTRITION FACTS

Calories: 207 | Carbohydrates: 5.7g | Fat: 14g | Protein: 15g | Cholesterol: 25mg

INGREDIENTS

- 3/4 cup orange juice
- 1 tablespoon ground cumin
- 1/2 cup lemon juice
- 1 tablespoon paprika
- 1/3 cup lime juice
- 1 teaspoon dried oregano
- 4 cloves garlic, minced
- 1 tablespoon black pepper
- 1/2 cup soy sauce
- 1 bunch fresh cilantro, chopped
- 1 teaspoon finely chopped canned chipotle pepper
- 1/2 cup olive oil
- 1 tablespoon chili powder
- 3 pounds flank steak

DIRECTIONS

1. Combine the orange, lemon, and lime juice in a large glass or ceramic bowl along with the garlic, soy sauce, chipotle pepper, chili power, ground cumin, paprika, dried oregano, black pepper, and cilantro. Slowly whisk in the olive oil until marinade is well combined. Remove one cup of the marinade and place in a small bowl, cover with plastic wrap and refrigerate for use after the meat is cooked.
2. Place the flank steak between two sheets of heavy plastic (resealable freezer bags work well) on a solid, level surface. Firmly pound the steak with the smooth side of a meat mallet to a thickness of 1/4 inch. After pounding, poke steak all over with a fork. Add the meat to the marinade in the large bowl, cover, and allow to marinate in the refrigerator for 24 hours.
3. Preheat an outdoor grill for medium-high heat, and lightly oil the grate.
4. Remove the steak from the marinade and grill to desired doneness, about 5 minutes per side for medium rare. Discard used marinade. Remove meat from heat and slice across the grain.
5. Pour the one cup of reserved, unused marinade over the hot meat and serve immediately.

DEE'S ROAST PORK FOR TACOS
Servings: 12 | Prep: 15m | Cooks: 4h | Total: 4h15m

NUTRITION FACTS

Calories: | Carbohydrates: g | Fat: g | Protein: g | Cholesterol: mg

INGREDIENTS

- 4 pounds pork shoulder roast
- 1 teaspoon taco seasoning
- 2 (4 ounce) cans diced green chilies, drained
- 2 teaspoons minced garlic
- 1/4 cup chili powder
- 1 1/2 teaspoons salt, or to taste
- 1 teaspoon dried oregano

DIRECTIONS

1. Combine rice and water in a medium saucepan. Bring to a boil over high heat. Reduce heat to low, cover with lid, and allow to steam until tender, about 20 minutes.
2. While rice is cooking, grind peanuts in a blender and set aside. Heat the margarine in a skillet over medium heat. Stir in the onion; cook and stir until the onion has softened and turned golden brown about 10 minutes. Stir in ginger, carrots, and salt to taste. Reduce heat to low and cover to steam 5 minutes. Stir in cayenne pepper and peanuts. When rice is done, add it to skillet and stir gently to combine with other ingredients. Garnish with chopped cilantro.

HOT MEXICAN SPINACH DIP
Servings: 56 | Prep: 15m | Cooks: 15m | Total: 30m

NUTRITION FACTS

Calories: 40 | Carbohydrates: 1.4g | Fat: 3.1g | Protein: 1.9g | Cholesterol: 9mg

INGREDIENTS

- 1 (16 ounce) jar salsa
- 1 cup evaporated milk
- 1 (10 ounce) package frozen chopped spinach, thawed and drained
- 1 (2.25 ounce) can chopped black olives, drained
- 2 cups shredded Monterey Jack cheese
- 1 tablespoon red wine vinegar
- 1 (8 ounce) package cream cheese, diced and softened
- salt and pepper to taste

DIRECTIONS

1. Preheat oven to 400 degrees F (200 degrees C).
2. In a medium baking dish, mix together salsa, chopped spinach, Monterey Jack cheese, cream cheese, evaporated milk, black olives, red wine vinegar, salt and pepper.
3. Bake mixture in the preheated oven 12 to 15 minutes, or until bubbly.

ENCHILADA CASSEROLE

Servings: 8 | Prep: 20m | Cooks: 35m | Total: 1h

NUTRITION FACTS

Calories: 449 | Carbohydrates: 34.6g | Fat: 22g | Protein: 28.4g | Cholesterol: 87mg

INGREDIENTS

- 1 (1.5 ounce) package dry enchilada sauce mix
- 1/2 teaspoon onion powder
- 1 (6 ounce) can tomato paste
- 1 (16 ounce) can refried beans
- 3/4 cup water
- 1 (12 ounce) package corn tortillas
- 1 1/2 pounds ground beef
- 1 cup shredded Cheddar cheese
- 1 teaspoon garlic salt
- 1 cup shredded Monterey Jack cheese

DIRECTIONS

1. Preheat oven to 375 degrees F (190 degrees C).
2. In a medium bowl, mix the dry enchilada sauce according to package directions, replacing tomato sauce with the tomato paste and water
3. In a large skillet, brown the ground beef with garlic salt and onion powder; drain fat. Mix refried beans and 1/2 cup of the prepared enchilada sauce with the meat.
4. Dip enough corn tortillas to cover the bottom of a 3 quart casserole dish in the remaining enchilada sauce. Arrange tortillas in the dish. Spoon in half of the meat mixture, covering the tortillas. Spread half of the Cheddar and Monterey Jack cheeses over the meat. Cover with another layer tortillas dipped in enchilada sauce. Spoon in remaining meat mixture and top with a final layer of tortillas dipped in enchilada sauce. Pour any remaining sauce over the layers and top with remaining cheese.
5. Cover and bake in preheated oven for 20 minutes. Remove from oven and let sit for 5 minutes before serving.

BAKED TORTILLA CHIPS

Servings: 6 | Prep: 10m | Cooks: 15m | Total: 25m

NUTRITION FACTS

Calories: 147 | Carbohydrates: 26g | Fat: 4.1g | Protein: 3.3g | Cholesterol: 0mg

INGREDIENTS

- 1 (12 ounce) package corn tortillas

- 1 teaspoon ground cumin
- 1 tablespoon vegetable oil
- 1 teaspoon chili powder
- 3 tablespoons lime juice
- 1 teaspoon salt

DIRECTIONS

1. Preheat oven to 350 degrees F (175 degrees C).
2. Cut each tortilla into 8 chip sized wedges and arrange the wedges in a single layer on a cookie sheet.
3. In a mister, combine the oil and lime juice. Mix well and spray each tortilla wedge until slightly moist.
4. Combine the cumin, chili powder and salt in a small bowl and sprinkle on the chips.
5. Bake for about 7 minutes. Rotate the pan and bake for another 8 minutes or until the chips are crisp, but not too brown. Serve with salsas, garnishes or guacamole.

TACO SALAD

Servings: 8 | Prep: 10m | Cooks: 30m | Total: 40m

NUTRITION FACTS

Calories: 846 | Carbohydrates: 59.6g | Fat: 56.5g | Protein: 26.1g | Cholesterol: 70mg

INGREDIENTS

- 1 pound lean ground beef
- 1 (14.5 ounce) package tortilla chips
- 1 (1.25 ounce) package taco seasoning mix
- 2 cups shredded Cheddar cheese
- 1 (16 ounce) can chili beans
- 1 cup chopped tomatoes
- 1 (16 ounce) bottle French dressing
- 4 tablespoons sour cream
- 1 head iceberg lettuce
- 1/2 cup prepared salsa

DIRECTIONS

1. In a large skillet over medium-high heat, brown the ground beef and drain excess fat. Stir in the taco seasoning, chili beans and French-style dressing. Fill the dressing bottle 2/3 full of water and add to the skillet. Bring to a boil, reduce heat and simmer for 15 minutes.
2. Crush the bag of chips, open the bag, and toss the broken chips into a large bowl with the lettuce, cheese and tomatoes. When the meat mixture is done, combine it with the lettuce, tomatoes, chips and mix well. Then, add salsa and sour cream.

VEGETARIAN MEXICAN INSPIRED STUFFED PEPPERS

Servings: 4 | Prep: 15m | Cooks: 40m | Total: 55m

NUTRITION FACTS

Calories: 509 | Carbohydrates: 55.5g | Fat: 22.8g | Protein: 23.8g | Cholesterol: 55mg

INGREDIENTS

- 1 tablespoon salt
- 1 (14.5 ounce) can chili-style diced tomatoes
- 4 large green bell peppers - tops, seeds, and membranes removed
- 1 teaspoon chili powder
- 1 tablespoon olive oil
- 1 teaspoon garlic salt
- 1/2 cup chopped onion
- 1/2 teaspoon ground cumin
- 2 cups cooked rice
- 1/2 teaspoon salt
- 1 (15 ounce) can black beans, drained and rinsed
- 1 (8 ounce) package shredded Mexican cheese blend (such as Sargento Authentic Mexican)

DIRECTIONS

1. Preheat oven to 350 degrees F (175 degrees C).
2. Bring a large pot of water and 1 tablespoon salt to a boil; cook green bell peppers in the boiling water until slightly softened, 3 to 4 minutes. Drain.
3. Heat olive oil in a skillet over medium heat; cook and stir onion in the hot oil until softened and transparent, 5 to 10 minutes.
4. Mix rice, black beans, tomatoes, and cooked onion in a large bowl. Add chili powder, garlic salt, cumin, 1/2 teaspoon salt; stir until evenly mixed. Fold 1 1/2 cups Mexican cheese blend into rice mixture. Spoon rice mixture into each bell pepper; arrange peppers in 9x9-inch baking dish. Sprinkle peppers with remaining Mexican cheese blend.
5. Bake in the preheated oven until cheese is melted and bubbling, about 30 minutes.

CHICKEN SUIZA CORNBREAD BAKE

Servings: 12 | Prep: 20m | Cooks: 40m | Total: 1h

NUTRITION FACTS

Calories: 378 | Carbohydrates: 30.1g | Fat: 21.8g | Protein: 17.9g | Cholesterol: 70mg

INGREDIENTS

- 1/2 cup butter

- 1 (15 ounce) can cream-style corn, drained
- 1 onion, finely chopped
- 1/4 teaspoon salt
- 1 clove garlic, minced
- 1/2 cup egg substitute
- 1 (15.25 ounce) can whole kernel corn, drained
- 1 (8.5 ounce) package corn bread mix

DIRECTIONS

1. Preheat oven to 375 degrees F (190 degrees C). Grease a 9x13-inch baking dish.
2. Melt butter in a small skillet over medium heat. Add onion and garlic; cook and stir until tender, 4 to 6 minutes (see Cook's Note). Remove from heat and set aside. In a large bowl, combine corn, cream-style corn, salt, and egg substitute. Beat in muffin mix. Fold in cooked onion mixture. Pour into prepared baking dish.
3. In a large bowl, combine chicken, green chiles, mushrooms, sour cream, salt and pepper. Spoon over corn mixture to within 1 inch from edge. Sprinkle top with cheese.
4. Bake in preheated oven for 35 to 40 minutes, or until edges are golden brown.

CHICKEN ENCIIILADA SOUP

Servings: 8 | Prep: 10m | Cooks: 50m | Total: 1h

NUTRITION FACTS

Calories: 290 | Carbohydrates: 13.8g | Fat: 16.3g | Protein: 22g | Cholesterol: 74mg

INGREDIENTS

- 1 pound skinless, boneless chicken breast halves
- 3 cups water, divided
- 1 tablespoon vegetable oil
- 1 cup enchilada sauce
- 1/2 cup diced onion
- 2 cups shredded Cheddar cheese
- 1 clove garlic, minced
- 1 teaspoon salt
- 1 quart chicken broth
- 1 teaspoon chili powder
- 1 cup masa harina
- 1/2 teaspoon ground cumin

DIRECTIONS

1. In a large pot over medium heat, cook chicken breasts in oil until well browned on all sides. Remove and set aside.
2. Cook onion and garlic in remaining oil until onions are translucent. Pour in chicken broth.
3. In a bowl, whisk together masa harina and 2 cups water until well blended. Pour into pot with remaining 1 cup water, enchilada sauce, Cheddar, salt, chili powder and cumin. Bring to a boil.
4. Shred cooked chicken and add it to the pot. Reduce heat and simmer 30 to 40 minutes, until thickened.

FARMER'S MARKET VEGETARIAN QUESADILLAS
Servings: 6 | Prep: 15m | Cooks: 15m | Total: 30m

NUTRITION FACTS

Calories: 209 | Carbohydrates: 36.8g | Fat: 7.1g | Protein: 10.2g | Cholesterol: 13mg

INGREDIENTS

- 1/2 cup chopped red bell pepper
- 1 tablespoon olive oil
- 1/2 cup chopped zucchini
- cooking spray
- 1/2 cup chopped yellow squash
- 6 (9 inch) whole wheat tortillas
- 1/2 cup chopped red onion
- 1 1/4 cups shredded reduced-fat sharp Cheddar cheese
- 1/2 cup chopped mushrooms

DIRECTIONS

1. In a large nonstick pan, cook red pepper, zucchini, yellow squash, onion, and mushrooms in olive oil over medium to medium-high heat for about 7 minutes, or until just tender. Remove vegetables from pan.
2. Coat the same pan with cooking spray, and place one tortilla in pan. Sprinkle 1/4 cup of cheese evenly over tortilla, and layer 3/4 cup of the vegetable mixture over the cheese. Sprinkle another 1/8 cup of cheese on the vegetables, and top with a second tortilla. Cook until golden on both sides, for approximately 2 to 3 minutes per side. Remove quesadilla from pan, and repeat with remaining ingredients. Cut each quesadilla into 8 triangles with a pizza cutter. Serve hot.

PORK CARNITAS
Servings: 12 | Prep: 15m | Cooks: 3h30m | Total: 3h45m

NUTRITION FACTS

Calories: 250 | Carbohydrates: 2.3g | Fat: 19.1g | Protein: 16.2g | Cholesterol: 62mg

INGREDIENTS

- 1/4 cup vegetable oil
- 3 tablespoons lime juice
- 4 pounds pork shoulder, cut into several large pieces
- 1 tablespoon chili powder
- 3 tablespoons kosher salt
- 1/2 teaspoon dried oregano
- 1 onion, chopped
- 1/2 teaspoon ground cumin
- 1 clove garlic, crushed
- 4 (14.5 ounce) cans chicken broth

DIRECTIONS

1. Heat the vegetable oil in a large Dutch oven over high heat. Season the pork shoulder with salt, then arrange the pork in the Dutch oven. Cook until browned on all sides, about 10 minutes. Add the onion, garlic, lime juice, chili powder, oregano, and cumin. Pour in the chicken broth, and bring to a boil. Reduce heat to medium-low, cover, and continue to simmer until pork is very tender, about 2 1/2 hours.
2. Preheat the oven to 400 degrees F (200 degrees C)
3. Transfer the pork shoulder to a large baking sheet, reserving the cooking liquid. Drizzle with a small amount of the reserved cooking liquid and lightly season with salt.
4. Bake the pork in the preheated oven until browned, about 30 minutes. Drizzle more of the cooking liquid on the meat every 10 minutes, and use two forks to shred the meat as it browns.

SEAFOOD ENCHILADAS

Servings: 6 | Prep: 15m | Cooks: 40m | Total: 55m

NUTRITION FACTS

Calories: 6.7 | Carbohydrates: 42.6g | Fat: 36.5g | Protein: 26.8g | Cholesterol: 136mg

INGREDIENTS

- 1 onion, chopped
- 1 cup half-and-half cream
- 1 tablespoon butter
- 1/2 cup sour cream
- 1/2 pound fresh crabmeat
- 1/4 cup butter, melted
- 1/4 pound shrimp - peeled, deveined and coarsely chopped
- 1 1/2 teaspoons dried parsley

- 8 ounces Colby cheese
- 1/2 teaspoon garlic salt
- 6 (10 inch) flour tortillas

DIRECTIONS

1. Preheat oven to 350 degrees F (175 degrees C).
2. In a large skillet, saute onions in 1 tablespoon butter until transparent. Remove the skillet from heat and stir in crabmeat and shrimp. Shred the cheese and mix half of it into the seafood. Place a large spoonful of the mixture into each tortilla. Roll the tortillas up around the mixture and arrange the rolled tortillas in a 9x13 inch baking dish.
3. In a saucepan over medium-low heat, combine half-and-half, sour cream, 1/4 cup butter, parsley and garlic salt. Stir until the mixture is lukewarm and blended. Pour sauce over the enchiladas, and sprinkle with remaining cheese.
4. Bake in preheated oven for 30 minutes.

MEXICAN STYLE SHREDDED PORK
Servings: 6 | Prep: 15m | Cooks: 7h | Total: 7h30m

NUTRITION FACTS

Calories: 520 | Carbohydrates: 43g | Fat: 19g | Protein: 41.1g | Cholesterol: 108mg

INGREDIENTS

- 1 (3 pound) boneless pork loin roast, cut into 2 inch pieces
- 3 1/4 cups water, divided
- 1/2 teaspoon salt
- 1 1/2 cups uncooked long grain white rice
- 2 (4 ounce) cans diced green chile peppers
- 1/4 cup fresh lime juice
- 3 cloves garlic, crushed
- 1/4 cup chopped cilantro
- 1/4 cup chipotle sauce

DIRECTIONS

1. Place the roast in a slow cooker, and season with salt. Place chile peppers and garlic on top of roast. Pour in the chipotle sauce and 1/2 cup water.
2. Cover, and cook 7 hours on Low.
3. In a pot, bring remaining 2 3/4 cups water and rice to a boil. Mix in the lime juice and cilantro. Reduce heat to low, cover, and simmer 20 minutes.
4. Remove roast from the slow cooker, and use two forks to shred. Return pork to the slow cooker, and allow to sit 15 minutes to absorb some of the liquid. Serve over the cooked rice.

SHREDDED BEEF ENCHILADAS

Servings: 10 | Prep: 45m | Cooks: 1h30m | Total: 2h15m

NUTRITION FACTS

Calories: 577 | Carbohydrates: 30.1g | Fat: 38g | Protein: 30g | Cholesterol: 112mg

INGREDIENTS

- 3 pounds beef chuck roast
- 2 (4 ounce) cans chopped green chile peppers
- 1/4 cup water
- 1 tablespoon all-purpose flour
- 1 1/2 cups beef broth
- 2 cups sour cream
- 3 tablespoons red wine vinegar
- 3 cups shredded Monterey Jack cheese, divided
- 2 tablespoons chili powder
- 1 cup oil for frying
- 1 tablespoon ground cumin
- 20 (6 inch) corn tortillas
- 1 large onion, chopped

DIRECTIONS

1. Place roast in a large saucepan that has a tight-fitting lid. Pour in water, cover, and simmer on low for 30 minutes. Increase heat to medium/high, and brown the roast on all sides. Once the water has boiled away, pour in the beef broth, vinegar, chili powder and 1 tablespoon of cumin. Cover tightly and reduce heat to low. Simmer for 1 1/2 to 2 hours or until the beef falls apart when you try to pick it up. Shred the beef, using 2 forks or your fingers. Place shredded beef back into the saucepan with all the juices, and let cool to room temperature.
2. In a large skillet, saute the onion until just soft, not browned. Mix in flour and green chilies. Stir constantly for 2 minutes to cook the flour taste out. Stir in sour cream and 2 cups of Monterey Jack cheese. Cook on low for 10 minutes, stirring often, until the cheese is all melted and mixed. Set aside and let cool.
3. In a large heavy skillet, heat the olive oil. Using tongs dip the tortillas, one at a time, into the oil for 30 seconds each side. Drain on paper towels.
4. Preheat oven to 375 degrees F (190 degrees C). Spread 4 tablespoons of sour cream mixture down the center of the tortilla. Top with about the same amount of beef. Roll up and place seam side down in one or two 8x11 inch baking dish. Repeat for each tortilla. Continue until you are out of the filling. Sprinkle with remaining Monterey Jack cheese.
5. Bake in a pre-heated oven for 30 minutes or until cheese is melted and bubbling.

CAMPBELL'S EASY CHICKEN AND CHEESE ENCHILADAS

Servings: 6 | Prep: 10m | Cooks: 40m | Total: 50m

NUTRITION FACTS

Calories: 456 | Carbohydrates: 45.9g | Fat: 19.4g | Protein: 23.2g | Cholesterol: 56mg

INGREDIENTS

- 1 (10.75 ounce) can Campbell's Condensed Cream of Chicken Soup (Regular, 98% Fat Free or Healthy Request)
- 1/2 cup shredded Monterey Jack cheese
- 1/2 cup sour cream
- 6 flour tortillas (6"), warmed
- 1 cup Pace Picante Sauce
- 1 small tomato, chopped
- 2 teaspoons chili powder
- 1 green onion, sliced
- 2 cups chopped cooked chicken
- 1/2 cup shredded Monterey Jack cheese

DIRECTIONS

1. Stir the soup, sour cream, picante sauce and chili powder in a medium bowl.
2. Stir 1 cup picante sauce mixture, chicken and cheese in a large bowl.
3. Divide the chicken mixture among the tortillas. Roll up the tortillas and place them seam side up in 11 x 8" shallow baking dish. Pour the remaining picante sauce mixture over the filled tortillas. Cover the baking dish.
4. Bake at 350 degrees F. for 40 min. or until the enchiladas are hot and bubbling. Top with the tomato and onion.

"PANTRY RAID" CHICKEN ENCHILADA CASSEROLE

Servings: 6 | Prep: 15m | Cooks: 45m | Total: 1h

NUTRITION FACTS

Calories: 487 | Carbohydrates: 45.9g | Fat: 19.8g | Protein: 31.2g | Cholesterol: 108mg

INGREDIENTS

- 1 (15 ounce) can tomato sauce
- 1 (15 ounce) can black beans, drained

- 1/4 cup water
- 1/4 cup cream cheese
- 1 envelope taco seasoning mix
- 1 cup shredded Mexican-style cheese blend, or more to taste
- 1 1/2 tablespoons chili powder
- 1 (7.5 ounce) package corn bread mix
- 1 tablespoon vegetable oil
- 1 egg
- 1 pound chicken breast tenderloins
- 1/3 cup milk

DIRECTIONS

1. Preheat the oven to 375 degrees F (190 degrees C). Grease a 9x9-inch baking dish.
2. Mix tomato sauce, water, taco seasoning mix, and chili powder together in a saucepan; bring to a simmer over medium heat.
3. Heat vegetable oil in a skillet over medium heat and brown chicken tenderloins on both sides, about 5 minutes per side. Pour tomato sauce mixture over the chicken, bring to a simmer, and cook over medium-low heat until chicken tenderloins are no longer pink inside, about 8 minutes. Transfer chicken to a bowl and shred; return shredded chicken to the sauce. Mix in black beans and cream cheese until thoroughly combined.
4. Pour chicken mixture into prepared baking dish. Top with shredded Mexican cheese. Whisk corn bread mix, egg, and milk in a bowl, and spoon the batter over the chicken mix
5. Bake in the preheated oven until the casserole is bubbling and the corn bread topping is browned and set, about 30 minutes.

BLACK BEAN SALAD

Servings: 12 | Prep: 20m | Cooks: 0m | Total: 20m

NUTRITION FACTS

Calories: 159 | Carbohydrates: 24.2g | Fat: 6.3g | Protein: 5g | Cholesterol: 0mg

INGREDIENTS

- 1 (15 ounce) can black beans, rinsed and drained
- 1 (4 ounce) jar pimentos
- 2 (15 ounce) cans whole kernel corn, drained
- 3 tomatoes, seeded and chopped
- 8 green onions, chopped
- 1 cup chopped fresh cilantro
- 2 jalapeno peppers, seeded and minced
- 1 lime, juiced

- 1 green bell pepper, chopped
- 1/2 cup Italian salad dressing
- 1 avocado - peeled, pitted, and diced
- 1/2 teaspoon garlic salt

DIRECTIONS

1. In a large bowl, combine the black beans, corn, green onions, jalapeno peppers, bell pepper, avocado, pimentos, tomatoes, cilantro, lime juice, and Italian dressing. Season with garlic salt. Toss, and chill until serving.

STUFFED MEXICAN PEPPERS

Servings: 6 | Prep: 15m | Cooks: 1h | Total: 1h15m

NUTRITION FACTS

Calories: 322 | Carbohydrates: 17.3g | Fat: 18.5g | Protein: 21.2g | Cholesterol: 73mg

INGREDIENTS

- 1 pound ground beef
- 1/4 teaspoon garlic salt
- 1 (1 ounce) package taco seasoning mix
- 1/8 teaspoon ground black pepper
- 3/4 cup water
- 2 (8 ounce) cans tomato sauce, divided
- 2 teaspoons chili powder
- 3 large red bell peppers
- 1/2 cup cooked rice
- 6 (1 inch) cubes Colby-Jack cheese
- 1/4 teaspoon salt

DIRECTIONS

1. Preheat oven to 350 degrees F (175 degrees C). Grease a 9x13-inch baking dish.
2. Place the ground beef into a skillet over medium heat, and brown the meat, breaking it apart into crumbles as it cooks, about 8 minutes. Drain excess fat. Stir in the taco seasoning, water, chili powder, cooked rice, salt, garlic salt, black pepper, and 1 can of tomato sauce; mix until thoroughly combined. Bring to a boil, reduce heat to low, and simmer 20 minutes.
3. Meanwhile, cut the bell peppers in half lengthwise, and remove stems, membranes, cores, and seeds. Place a steamer insert into a large saucepan, and fill with water to just below the bottom of the steamer. Cover, and bring the water to a boil over high heat. Place the peppers into the steamer insert, cover the pan, and steam until just tender, 3 to 5 minutes.

4. Place the steamed peppers into the prepared baking dish, and fill lightly with the meat filling. Press 1 cube of Colby-Jack cheese into the center of the filling in each pepper, and spoon the remaining can of tomato sauce over the peppers. Cover the dish with aluminum foil.
5. Bake in the preheated oven until the peppers are tender and the filling is hot, 25 to 30 minutes.

HEATHER'S CILANTRO, BLACK BEAN, AND CORN SALSA
Servings: 72 | Prep: 25m | Cooks: 0m | Total: 25m

NUTRITION FACTS

Calories: 30 | Carbohydrates: 4.9g | Fat: 0.9g | Protein: 1.1g | Cholesterol: 0mg

INGREDIENTS

- 1 (15 ounce) can yellow corn, drained
- 1 small red onion, finely chopped
- 1 (15 ounce) can white corn, drained
- 1 red bell pepper, seeded and chopped
- 2 (15 ounce) cans black beans, drained and rinsed
- 1 tablespoon minced garlic
- 1 (14.5 ounce) can Italian-style diced tomatoes, drained
- 1/4 cup lime juice
- 1 bunch finely chopped cilantro
- 1 avocado - peeled, pitted, and diced
- 5 green onions, finely sliced
- 2 tablespoons olive oil, or to taste

DIRECTIONS

1. Stir the yellow and white corn, black beans, tomatoes, cilantro, green onion, red onion, bell pepper, and garlic in a large bowl. Gently mix in the lime juice and avocado. Drizzle with olive oil to serve.

FISH TACOS WITH HONEY-CUMIN CILANTRO SLAW AND CHIPOTLE MAYO
Servings: 4 | Prep: 30m | Cooks: 10m | Total: 4h40m

NUTRITION FACTS

Calories: 984 | Carbohydrates: 117.5g | Fat: 44.4g | Protein: 42.2g | Cholesterol: 137mg

INGREDIENTS

- 1 pound tilapia fillets, cut into chunks

- 1/8 teaspoon cayenne pepper
- 1/2 cup fresh lime juice
- 1/3 cup all-purpose flour
- 1/3 cup fresh lime juice
- 2 eggs, lightly beaten
- 2 tablespoons honey
- 2 cups panko crumbs
- 1 tablespoon vegetable oil
- salt and ground black pepper to taste
- 1 teaspoon ground cumin
- 1 cup vegetable oil for frying
- 1/2 cup mayonnaise
- 2 cups 3 color coleslaw blend
- 2 chipotle chilies in adobo sauce
- 1 cup minced fresh cilantro leaves
- 1 tablespoon adobo sauce from chipotle peppers
- 8 (7 inch) flour tortillas, warmed
- 1/4 teaspoon salt

DIRECTIONS

1. Place the tilapia chunks in a flat dish and pour 1/2 cup lime juice over the fish. Cover, and refrigerate at least 4 hours.
2. Meanwhile, make the honey-cumin sauce by whisking together 1/3 cup lime juice, honey, vegetable oil, and ground cumin a small bowl. Set aside until needed.
3. To make the chipotle mayonnaise dressing, place the mayonnaise, chilies, adobo sauce, 1/4 teaspoon salt, and cayenne pepper together in the bowl of a food processor. Pulse until smooth. Cover, and refrigerate until needed.
4. To bread the fish, place the flour, eggs, and panko crumbs in three separate shallow dishes. Season the fish with salt and pepper to taste. Dip the fish pieces first in the four, coating evenly, and shaking off any excess. Dip next in the eggs, and last in the panko crumbs, patting the pieces to help the breadcrumbs hold. Set the fish aside on a plate.
5. To cook the breaded fish, pour 1 cup vegetable oil into a skillet to 1/4 inch deep. Heat the oil to 365 degrees F (185 degrees C) over medium heat. Cook the fish, turning until all sides are golden brown, and flesh is easily flaked with a fork. Drain on paper towels. Brush the fish with the honey-cumin sauce.
6. Mix the coleslaw and cilantro together in a bowl. Reserve 1/4 cup of the chipotle mayonnaise dressing, and pour the remaining dressing over the coleslaw mixture. Toss to coat evenly with the dressing.
7. Place the tortillas on a flat surface, and spread each with 1 tablespoon reserved chipotle mayonnaise dressing. Divide the fish between the tortillas. Top with the cilantro coleslaw.

AUTHENTIC MEXICAN TORTILLAS
Servings: 12 | Prep: 30m | Cooks: 25m | Total: 55m

NUTRITION FACTS

Calories: 227 | Carbohydrates: 24.1g | Fat: 13.1g | Protein: 3.2g | Cholesterol: 0mg

INGREDIENTS

- 3 cups all-purpose flour
- 3/4 cup shortening
- 2 teaspoons baking powder
- 3/4 cup hot water
- 2 teaspoons salt

DIRECTIONS

1. Combine the flour, baking powder, and salt. Either by hand or with a pastry cutter, cut in the shortening till the mixture is crumbly. If the mixture looks more floury than crumbly, be sure to add just one or two more tablespoons of shortening till it is crumbly. Add about 3/4 cup hot water to the mixture, or just enough to make the ingredients look moist. Watch Now
2. With your hand or a large fork, knead the mixture making sure to rub the dough against the sides of the large mixing bowl to gather any clinging dough. If the dough still sticks to the side of the bowl, add a couple more tablespoons of flour until the dough forms a soft round shape. The dough is ready to roll out now, but it is best to let it rest. Cover it with a dish towel, and let it sit for about an hour or so. Watch Now
3. Take the dough, and pull it apart into 10 to 12 balls. Lightly flour your rolling area, and roll each ball with a rolling pin to about 1/8 inch thickness. Watch Now
4. Place each tortilla on a medium hot cast iron skillet. Cook for about 1 to 2 minutes on each side, or until the tortilla does not look doughy. Watch Now.

HOMEMADE TACO SEASONING MIX

Servings: 4 | Prep: 5m | Cooks: 0m | Total: 5m

NUTRITION FACTS

Calories: 12 | Carbohydrates: 2.4g | Fat: 0.5g | Protein: 0.5g | Cholesterol: 0mg

INGREDIENTS

- 2 teaspoons hot chili powder
- 1/2 teaspoon ground cumin
- 1 1/2 teaspoons paprika
- 1/2 teaspoon oregano
- 1 teaspoon onion powder
- 1/4 teaspoon freshly ground black pepper, or to taste
- 1/2 teaspoon sea salt
- 1 pinch cayenne pepper, or to taste (optional)
- 1/2 teaspoon garlic powder

- 1 pinch red pepper flakes, or to taste (optional)

DIRECTIONS

1. Mix chili powder, paprika, onion powder, sea salt, garlic powder, cumin, oregano, black pepper, cayenne pepper, and red pepper flakes in a bowl.

JALAPENO CREAM CHEESE CHICKEN ENCHILADAS
Servings: 7 | Prep: 25m | Cooks: 1h15m | Total: 1h40m

NUTRITION FACTS

Calories: 583 | Carbohydrates: 38.4g | Fat: 35.5g | Protein: 28.7g | Cholesterol: 123mg

INGREDIENTS

- 3 skinless, boneless chicken breast halves
- 1 tablespoon garlic powder
- 1 teaspoon cayenne pepper
- 1/2 teaspoon cayenne pepper
- 1/2 teaspoon garlic powder
- ½ teaspoon paprika
- salt and ground black pepper to taste
- 1/2 teaspoon chili powder
- 2 tablespoons butter
- 1/2 teaspoon ground cumin
- 1 large onion, minced
- 1 (28 ounce) can green enchilada sauce
- 2 jalapeno peppers, seeded and minced (wear gloves)
- 7 flour tortillas
- 1 (8 ounce) package cream cheese
- 8 ounces shredded Monterey Jack cheese, divided

DIRECTIONS

1. Preheat oven to 350 degrees F (175 degrees C).
2. Season chicken breasts with 1 teaspoon of cayenne pepper, 1/2 teaspoon of garlic powder, salt, and black pepper. Place into a baking dish.
3. Bake in the preheated oven until the chicken is no longer pink inside and the juices run clear, about 45 minutes. Allow chicken to cool, and shred with 2 forks. Set chicken aside.

4. Heat butter in a large nonstick skillet over medium heat, and cook the onion and jalapenos until the onion is translucent, about 5 minutes; stir in the cream cheese in chunks, and allow cream cheese to melt and soften. Stir in cream cheese, garlic powder, cayenne pepper, paprika, chili powder, and cumin. Mix in the cooked chicken meat; remove from heat.

5. Pour half the green enchilada sauce into the bottom of a 9x13-inch baking dish. Lay tortillas out onto a work surface, and place chicken mixture in a line down the center of each tortilla; sprinkle with about 1 tablespoon of Monterey Jack cheese per tortilla. Roll up the tortillas, and place into the sauce in the dish, seam sides down; pour the remaining sauce over the enchiladas. Sprinkle remaining 4 ounces of Monterey Jack cheese over the top.

6. Bake in the preheated oven until the filling is hot and bubbling and the cheese has melted, 30 to 35 minutes.

MEXICAN SHEPHERD'S PIE

Servings: 8 | Prep: 20m | Cooks: 40m | Total: 1h

NUTRITION FACTS

Calories: 407 | Carbohydrates: 33.9g | Fat: 19.8g | Protein: 22.6g | Cholesterol: 71mg

INGREDIENTS

- 1 1/2 pounds ground beef
- 3/4 cup hot water
- 1 onion, finely chopped
- 1 (11 ounce) can whole kernel corn, drained
- garlic powder to taste
- 1 (8.5 ounce) package corn muffin mix
- salt and pepper to taste
- 1 cup shredded Cheddar cheese (optional)
- 1 (14.5 ounce) can diced tomatoes
- 1 (2.25 ounce) can sliced black olives (optional)
- 1 (1.25 ounce) package taco seasoning mix

DIRECTIONS

1. Preheat oven to 400 degrees F (200 degrees C). Spray a 9x13 inch baking dish with cooking spray.
2. Place the beef and onion in a skillet over medium heat. Cook until beef is evenly brown and onion is tender. Drain grease. Season with garlic powder, salt, and pepper. Mix in the tomatoes, and cook 5 minutes. Stir in the taco seasoning and water. Bring to a boil, reduce heat to low, and continue cooking 5 minutes, until thickened. Transfer to the prepared baking dish, and top evenly with corn.
3. Prepare the corn muffin mix according to package directions. Spread evenly over the corn layer in the baking dish.
4. Bake 20 minutes in the preheated oven, or until puffed and golden. Garnish with olives and cheese.

BEAN QUESADILLAS

Servings: 12 | Prep: 15m | Cooks: 30m | Total: 45m

NUTRITION FACTS

Calories: 504 | Carbohydrates: 69.7g | Fat: 18.3g | Protein: 14.7g | Cholesterol: 10mg

INGREDIENTS

- 1 tablespoon vegetable oil
- 2 tomatoes, chopped
- 1 onion, finely diced
- 1/2 (10 ounce) package frozen corn
- 2 cloves garlic, minced
- 12 (12 inch) flour tortillas
- 1 (15 ounce) can black beans, rinsed and drained
- 1 cup shredded Cheddar cheese
- 1 green bell pepper, chopped
- 1/4 cup vegetable oil

DIRECTIONS

1. Heat 1 tablespoon oil in a skillet over medium heat, and saute the onion and garlic until soft. Mix in beans, bell pepper, tomatoes, and corn; cook until heated through.
2. Spread 6 tortillas with equal amounts of the bean and vegetable mixture. Sprinkle with equal amounts of the Cheddar cheese, and top with the remaining tortillas to form quesadillas.
3. Heat 1/4 cup oil in a large skillet over medium-high heat. Place quesadillas in the skillet and cook, turning once, until cheese is melted and both sides are lightly browned.

TERRY'S TEXAS PINTO BEANS

Servings: 8 | Prep: 15m | Cooks: 2h | Total: 2h15m

NUTRITION FACTS

Calories: 210 | Carbohydrates: 37.9g | Fat: 1.1g | Protein: 13.2g | Cholesterol: 1mg

INGREDIENTS

- 1 pound dry pinto beans
- 1/2 cup green salsa
- 1 (29 ounce) can reduced sodium chicken broth
- 1 teaspoon cumin
- 1 large onion, chopped
- 1/2 teaspoon ground black pepper

- 1 fresh jalapeno pepper, chopped
- water, if needed
- 2 cloves garlic, minced

DIRECTIONS

1. Place the pinto beans in a large pot, and pour in the chicken broth. Stir in onion, jalapeno, garlic, salsa, cumin, and pepper. Bring to a boil, reduce heat to medium-low, and continue cooking 2 hours, stirring often, until beans are tender. Add water as needed to keep the beans moist.

ENCHILADAS

Servings: 8 | Prep: 20m | Cooks: 30m | Total:50 m

NUTRITION FACTS

Calories: 755 | Carbohydrates: 48.5g | Fat: 46g | Protein: 36.3g | Cholesterol: 150mg

INGREDIENTS

- 2 pounds lean ground beef
- 2 teaspoons vegetable oil
- 1 large chopped onion
- 8 ounces shredded Colby cheese
- 1/8 teaspoon garlic salt
- 2 (19 ounce) cans enchilada sauce
- 12 (8 inch) flour tortillas

DIRECTIONS

1. Preheat oven to 350 degrees F (175 degrees C).
2. In a heavy saucepan or skillet, brown the ground beef and onions. Season the ground beef mixture with garlic salt and set aside.
3. In a skillet, fry the tortillas in vegetable oil. Spoon some meat mixture and cheese into the center of each tortilla, roll them up and arrange them in a 9x13 inch baking dish or oblong pan. Pour the enchilada sauce over the rolled enchiladas and top with any remaining meat or cheese.
4. Bake in the preheated 350 degrees F (175 degrees C) for 20 to 30 minutes.

RONALDO'S BEEF CARNITAS

Servings: 12 | Prep: 10m | Cooks: 4h | Total: 4h10m

NUTRITION FACTS

Calories: 218 | Carbohydrates: 1.4g | Fat: 13.8g | Protein: 20.8g | Cholesterol: 70mg

INGREDIENTS

- 4 pounds chuck roast
- 1/2 teaspoon ground cumin
- 1 (4 ounce) can green chile peppers, chopped
- 2 cloves garlic, minced
- 2 tablespoons chili powder
- salt to taste
- 1/2 teaspoon dried oregano

DIRECTIONS

1. Preheat oven to 300 degrees F (150 degrees C).
2. Place roast on heavy foil large enough to enclose the meat. In a small bowl, combine the green chile peppers, chili powder, oregano, cumin, garlic and salt to taste. Mix well and rub over the meat.
3. Totally wrap the meat in the foil and place in a roasting pan.
4. Bake at 300 degrees F (150 degrees C) for 3 1/2 to 4 hours, or until the roast just falls apart with a fork. Remove from oven and shred using two forks.

TACO DIP

Servings: 25 | Prep: 10m | Cooks: 0m | Total: 10m

NUTRITION FACTS

Calories: 78 | Carbohydrates: 5.2g | Fat: 4.9g | Protein: 2.6g | Cholesterol: 17mg

INGREDIENTS

- 1 (8 ounce) package cream cheese, softened
- 1 cup shredded Cheddar cheese
- 1 (16 ounce) container nonfat sour cream
- 3 chopped tomatoes
- 1 (1.25 ounce) package taco seasoning mix
- 1 green bell pepper, chopped
- 1/4 head iceberg lettuce - rinsed, dried, and shred
- 1 (2.25 ounce) can black olives, drained

DIRECTIONS

1. In a medium-sized mixing bowl, combine cream cheese, sour cream and taco seasoning. Spread this mixture in a 9-inch (or a little larger) round serving dish. Top the mixture with lettuce, Cheddar cheese, tomatoes, bell pepper and black olives.

VEGAN BEAN TACO FILLING

Servings: 8 | Prep: 15m | Cooks: 15m | Total: 30m

NUTRITION FACTS

Calories: 142 | Carbohydrates: 24g | Fat: 2.5g | Protein: 7.5g | Cholesterol: 0mg

INGREDIENTS

- 1 tablespoon olive oil
- 1 1/2 tablespoons cumin
- 1 onion, diced
- 1 teaspoon paprika
- 2 cloves garlic, minced
- 1 teaspoon cayenne pepper
- 1 bell pepper, chopped
- 1 teaspoon chili powder
- 2 (14.5 ounce) cans black beans, rinsed, drained, and mashed
- 1 cup salsa
- 2 tablespoons yellow cornmeal

DIRECTIONS

- Heat olive oil in a medium skillet over medium heat. Stir in onion, garlic, and bell pepper; cook until tender. Stir in mashed beans. Add the cornmeal. Mix in cumin, paprika, cayenne, chili powder, and salsa. Cover, and cook 5 minutes. Watch Now.

MARGARITA CAKE

Servings: 12 | Prep: 10m | Cooks: 1h | Total: 1h20m | Additional: 10m

NUTRITION FACTS

Calories: 393 | Carbohydrates: 53.7g | Fat: g | Protein: 4g | Cholesterol: 63mg

INGREDIENTS

- 1 (18.25 ounce) package orange cake mix
- 1/4 cup tequila
- 1 (3.4 ounce) package instant vanilla pudding mix
- 2 tablespoons triple sec liqueur
- 4 eggs
- 1 cup confectioners' sugar
- 1/2 cup vegetable oil
- 1 tablespoon tequila

- 2/3 cup water
- 2 tablespoons triple sec liqueur
- 1/4 cup lemon juice
- 2 tablespoons lime juice

DIRECTIONS

1. Preheat oven to 350 degrees F (175 degrees C). Grease and flour a 10 inch Bundt pan.
2. In a large bowl combine cake mix, pudding mix, eggs, oil, water, lemon juice 1/4 cup tequila and 2 tablespoons triple sec. Beat for 2 minutes.
3. Pour batter into prepared pan. Bake in the preheated oven for 45 to 50 minutes, or until a toothpick inserted into the center of the cake comes out clean. Cool in pan for 10 minutes; remove to rack and pour glaze over cake while still warm.
4. To make the glaze: In a small bowl, combine confectioners' sugar with 1 tablespoon tequila, 2 tablespoons triple sec and 2 tablespoons lime juice. Mix until smooth.

CHICKEN TORTILLA SOUP
Servings: 6 | Prep: 15m | Cooks: 55m | Total: 1h10m

NUTRITION FACTS

Calories: 418 | Carbohydrates: 24.4g | Fat: 22.3g | Protein: 29.2g | Cholesterol: 69mg

INGREDIENTS

- 6 tablespoons vegetable oil
- 1 tablespoon chili powder
- 8 (6 inch) corn tortillas, coarsely chopped
- 3 bay leaves
- 6 cloves garlic, minced
- 6 cups chicken broth
- 1/2 cup chopped fresh cilantro
- 1 teaspoon salt
- 1 onion, chopped
- 1/2 teaspoon ground cayenne pepper
- 1 (29 ounce) can diced tomatoes
- 5 boneless chicken breast halves, cooked
- 2 tablespoons ground cumin

DIRECTIONS

1. In a large stock pot heat oil. Add tortillas, garlic, cilantro and onion. Saute for 2 to 3 minutes.

2. Stir in tomatoes and bring to a boil. Add cumin, chili powder, bay leaves and chicken stock. Return to a boil, reduce heat to medium and add salt and cayenne. Simmer for 30 minutes remove bay leaves and stir in chicken. Heat through and serve.

CHICKEN WITH CHIPOTLE
Servings: 8 | Prep: 5m | Cooks: 50m | Total: 55m

NUTRITION FACTS

Calories: 362 | Carbohydrates: 3.9g | Fat: 23.6g | Protein: 31.7g | Cholesterol: 119mg

INGREDIENTS

- 8 chicken leg quarters
- 2 tablespoons chicken bouillon granules
- 1 1/2 cups milk
- 1 tablespoon margarine
- 1 cup sour cream
- salt to taste
- 2 chipotle peppers in adobo sauce

DIRECTIONS

1. Preheat oven to 375 degrees F (190 degrees C).
2. Roast the chicken legs in the preheated oven until the skin is crispy, and the meat is cooked through, 30 to 40 minutes.
3. While the chicken is roasting, puree the milk, sour cream, chipotle peppers, and chicken bouillon granules in a blender until smooth. Melt the margarine in a large pan over medium heat. Pour in the chipotle puree, bring to a simmer, reduce heat to low, and season with salt to taste. Add the cooked chicken legs, and simmer for about 10 minutes, until chicken has taken on the flavor of the sauce.

SPINACH ENCHILADAS VERDE
Servings: 6 | Prep: 15m | Cooks: 20m | Total: 35m

NUTRITION FACTS

Calories: 321 | Carbohydrates: 27.1g | Fat: 17.8g | Protein: 14.7g | Cholesterol: 49mg

INGREDIENTS

- 1 cup light sour cream
- 2 cups shredded Monterey Jack cheese
- 1 (7 ounce) can green salsa
- 1 (10 ounce) package corn tortillas

- 1 bunch fresh spinach, rinsed and thinly sliced

DIRECTIONS

1. Preheat the oven to 350 degrees F (175 degrees C).
2. In a small bowl, stir together half of the sour cream and the green salsa. Spread enough to coat the bottom into a 9x13 inch baking dish. On each tortilla, spread a small amount of the salsa and sour cream in the center. Lay a small handful of spinach over that, and sprinkle with Monterey Jack cheese. Roll up, secure with a toothpick and place into the baking dish. When all of the tortillas are in the pan, pour the remaining salsa over the top and sprinkle with the remaining cheese.
3. Bake for 20 to 25 minutes in the preheated oven, until the enchiladas are browned and heated through.

ONE SKILLET MEXICAN QUINOA
Servings: 4 | Prep: 15m | Cooks: 25m | Total: 40m

NUTRITION FACTS

Calories: 450 | Carbohydrates: 67.1g | Fat: 14.9g | Protein: 16.5g | Cholesterol: 2mg

INGREDIENTS

- 1 tablespoon olive oil
- 1 tablespoon red pepper flakes, or to taste
- 1 jalapeno pepper, chopped
- 1 1/2 teaspoons chili powder
- 2 cloves garlic, chopped
- 1/2 teaspoon cumin
- 1 (15 ounce) can black beans, rinsed and drained
- 1 pinch kosher salt and ground black pepper to taste
- 1 (14.5 ounce) can fire-roasted diced tomatoes
- 1 avocado - peeled, pitted, and diced
- 1 cup yellow corn
- 1 lime, juiced
- 1 cup quinoa
- 2 tablespoons chopped fresh cilantro
- 1 cup chicken broth

DIRECTIONS

1. Heat oil in a large skillet over medium-high heat. Saute jalapeno pepper and garlic in hot oil until fragrant, about 1 minute.
2. Stir black beans, tomatoes, yellow corn, quinoa, and chicken broth into skillet; season with red pepper flakes, chili powder, cumin, salt, and black pepper. Bring to a boil, cover the skillet with a

lid, reduce heat to low, and simmer until quinoa is tender and liquid is mostly absorbed, about 20 minutes. Stir avocado, lime juice, and cilantro into quinoa until combined.

ACAPULCO CHICKEN
Servings: 2 | Prep: 10m | Cooks: 15m | Total: 25m

NUTRITION FACTS

Calories: 333 | Carbohydrates: 23.8g | Fat: 13.9g | Protein: 30.1g | Cholesterol: 72mg

INGREDIENTS

- 2 skinless, boneless chicken breast halves - cut into bite-size pieces
- 1/2 cup chopped onion
- 1 tablespoon chili powder, divided
- 2 jalapeno peppers, seeded and minced
- salt and pepper to taste
- 1 large tomato, cut into chunks
- 1 tablespoon olive oil
- 10 drops hot pepper sauce
- 1 cup chopped green bell pepper

DIRECTIONS

1. Season chicken with 1/2 tablespoon chili powder, salt and pepper. Heat oil in a large skillet over medium high heat and saute seasoned chicken for 3 to 4 minutes, or until no longer pink. Remove from skillet with a slotted spoon and keep warm.
2. In same skillet, stir fry bell pepper and onion until soft. Add jalapeno peppers, tomatoes, remaining 1/2 tablespoon chili powder and hot pepper sauce. Cook, stirring, for an additional 3 to 5 minutes; add chicken and stir fry for 2 minutes more.

SEVEN LAYER DIP
Servings: 64 | Prep: 20m | Cooks: 0m | Total: 20m

NUTRITION FACTS

Calories: 42 | Carbohydrates: 2.8g | Fat: 2.9g | Protein: 1.5g | Cholesterol: 5mg

INGREDIENTS

- 2 avocados - peeled, pitted and diced
- 1 (1 ounce) package taco seasoning mix
- 1 1/2 tablespoons fresh lime juice
- 4 roma (plum) tomatoes, diced

- 1/4 cup chopped fresh cilantro
- 1 bunch green onions, finely chopped
- 1/4 cup salsa
- 1 (16 ounce) can refried beans
- garlic salt to taste
- 2 cups shredded Mexican-style cheese blend
- ground black pepper to taste
- 1 (2.25 ounce) can black olives - drained and finely chopped
- 1 (8 ounce) container sour cream

DIRECTIONS

1. In a medium bowl, mash the avocados. Mix in lime juice, cilantro, salsa, garlic salt and pepper.
2. In a small bowl, blend the sour cream and taco seasoning.
3. In a 9x13 inch dish or on a large serving platter, spread the refried beans. Top with sour cream mixture. Spread on guacamole. Top with tomatoes, green onions, Mexican-style cheese blend and black olives.

TRES LECHES CAKE

Servings: 8 | Prep: 25m | Cooks: 45m | Total: 2h30m | Additional: 1h20m

NUTRITION FACTS

Calories: 642 | Carbohydrates: 75g | Fat: 33 | Protein: 14.2g | Cholesterol: 241mg

INGREDIENTS

- aspoons baking powder
- 1 pint heavy whipping cream
- 1 (14 ounce) can sweetened condensed milk
- 10 maraschino cherries
- 1 (12 fluid ounce) can evaporated milk

DIRECTIONS

1. Preheat oven to 350 degrees F (175 degrees C). Butter and flour bottom of a 9-inch springform pan.
2. Beat the egg yolks with 3/4 cup sugar until light in color and doubled in volume. Stir in milk, vanilla, flour and baking powder.
3. In a small bowl, beat egg whites until soft peaks form. Gradually add remaining 1/4 cup sugar. Beat until firm but not dry. Fold 1/3 of the egg whites into the yolk mixture to lighten it; fold in remaining egg whites. Pour batter into prepared pan.

4. Bake in preheated oven for 45 to 50 minutes or until cake tester inserted into the middle comes out clean. Allow to cool 10 minutes.
5. Loosen edge of cake with knife before removing side of pan. Cool cake completely on a wire rack.
6. Place cooled cake on a deep serving plate. Use a two-pronged meat fork or a cake tester to pierce the surface of cake.
7. Mix together condensed milk, evaporated milk and 1/4 cup of the whipping cream. Set aside 1 cup of the measured milk mixture and refrigerate for another use. Pour remaining milk mixture over cake slowly until absorbed. Whip the remaining whipping cream until it thickens and reaches spreading consistency. Frost cake with whipped cream and garnish with cherries. Store cake in the refrigerator.

MEXICAN CORN
Servings: 6 | Prep: 10m | Cooks: 10m | Total: 20m

NUTRITION FACTS

Calories: 359 | Carbohydrates: 38.2g | Fat: 22.7g | Protein: 8g | Cholesterol: 61mg

INGREDIENTS

- 2 (15.25 ounce) cans whole kernel corn, drained
- 10 jalapeno peppers, chopped
- 1 (8 ounce) package cream cheese
- 1 teaspoon garlic salt
- 1/4 cup butter

DIRECTIONS

1. In a medium saucepan combine corn, cream cheese, butter, jalapeno peppers and garlic salt. Cook over medium heat for about 10 minutes or until heated through, stirring constantly after cream cheese begins to melt.

APPLE ENCHILADAS
Servings: 6 | Prep: 10m | Cooks: 30m | Total: 1h

NUTRITION FACTS

Calories: 530 | Carbohydrates: 88.2g | Fat: 18.9g | Protein: 4.6g | Cholesterol: 41mg

INGREDIENTS

- 1 (21 ounce) can apple pie filling
- 1/2 cup white sugar
- 6 (8 inch) flour tortillas
- 1/2 cup brown sugar

- 1 teaspoon ground cinnamon
- 1/2 cup water
- 1/2 cup butter

DIRECTIONS

1. Preheat oven to 350 degrees F (175 degrees C). Grease a 2 quart baking dish.
2. Spoon about one heaping quarter cup of pie filling evenly down the center of each tortilla. Sprinkle with cinnamon; roll up, tucking in edges; and place seam side down in prepared dish.
3. In a medium saucepan over medium heat, combine butter, white sugar, brown sugar and water. Bring to a boil, stirring constantly; reduce heat and simmer 3 minutes. Pour sauce over enchiladas and let stand 30 minutes.
4. Bake in preheated oven 20 minutes, or until golden.

CHICKEN ENCHILADA SLOW COOKER SOUP
Servings: 6 | Prep: 15m | Cooks: 6h30m | Total: 6h45m

NUTRITION FACTS

Calories: 186 | Carbohydrates: 22.9g | Fat: 3.4g | Protein: 18.4g | Cholesterol: 39mg

INGREDIENTS

- 1 pound skinless, boneless chicken breast halves
- 1/4 cup chopped fresh cilantro
- 1 (15.25 ounce) can whole kernel corn, drained
- 2 bay leaves
- 1 (14.5 ounce) can diced tomatoes including juice
- 3 cloves garlic, minced
- 1 (14.5 ounce) can chicken broth
- 1 teaspoon ground cumin
- 1 (10 ounce) can enchilada sauce
- 1 teaspoon chili powder
- 1 (4 ounce) can diced green chiles
- 1 teaspoon salt
- 1 white onion, chopped
- 1/4 teaspoon ground black pepper, or to taste

DIRECTIONS

1. Rinse and pat dry the chicken breasts, then place into the bottom of a slow cooker. Add the corn, tomatoes, chicken broth, enchilada sauce, green chiles, onion, cilantro, bay leaves, garlic, cumin, chili powder, salt, and black pepper.
2. Cook on Low for 6 hours. Transfer the chicken to a large plate, then shred the meat with two forks. Return the chicken to the slow cooker and continue cooking for 30 minutes to 1 hour.

CHICKEN FAJITA MELTS

Servings: 8 | Prep: 10m | Cooks: 25m | Total: 35m

NUTRITION FACTS

Calories: 397 | Carbohydrates: 19.9g | Fat: 16.6g | Protein: 40.3g | Cholesterol: 104mg

INGREDIENTS

- 3 tablespoons vegetable oil
- 2 tablespoons taco seasoning mix
- 6 (6 ounce) skinless, boneless chicken breast halves, thinly sliced
- 1 cup salsa
- 1/2 cup sliced onions
- 8 (1/2 inch thick) slices French bread
- 1/2 cup sliced red bell pepper
- 2 cups shredded Cheddar cheese
- 1/2 cup tomato juice

DIRECTIONS

1. Heat the oil in a large skillet over medium-high heat. Add the chicken, and cook and stir until lightly browned, about 5 minutes.
2. Stir in the sliced onions and red peppers, and cook and stir for 5 minutes or until the vegetables are tender. Stir in the tomato juice and taco seasoning, and mix well. Cook mixture until the juice has thickened and the chicken is well coated with sauce, about an additional 7 minutes.
3. Preheat the oven's broiler and set the oven rack about 6 inches from the heat source.
4. Spread 2 tablespoons of salsa over each slice of French bread. Evenly spoon the chicken mixture on top of the salsa topped bread. Sprinkle each sandwich with 1/4 cup Cheddar cheese.
5. Place sandwiches under the preheated broiler and cook for 5 minutes or until the cheese is melted and beginning to brown.

CHICKEN CHIMI IN THE OVEN

Servings: 6 | Prep: 25m | Cooks: 25m | Total: 50m

NUTRITION FACTS

Calories: 510 | Carbohydrates: 52.5g | Fat: g | Protein: 33.8g | Cholesterol: 68mg

INGREDIENTS

- 4 tablespoons olive oil, divided
- 1/2 teaspoon ground cumin
- 1/2 cup chopped onion

- 1/2 teaspoon ground cinnamon
- 2 cloves garlic, minced
- 1 pound cooked, shredded chicken breast meat
- 2 cups salsa
- 1 cup refried beans
- 3 tablespoons water
- 6 (10 inch) flour tortillas
- 1/4 cup chili powder

DIRECTIONS

1. Preheat oven to 425 degrees F (220 degrees C). Lightly grease a medium baking dish.
2. Heat 2 tablespoons oil in a large saucepan over medium heat. Saute onion and garlic in oil until tender. Stir in salsa and water. Season with chili powder, cumin, and cinnamon. Transfer the mixture to a blender or food processor, and blend until smooth. Return mixture to the saucepan, stir in the chicken, and cook until heated through.
3. Spoon an equal amount of refried beans down center of each tortilla, and top with equal amounts of the chicken mixture. Fold tortillas over the filling, and secure with toothpicks. Arrange seam-side down in the prepared baking dish, and brush with the remaining olive oil
4. Bake 15 minutes in the preheated oven, turning every 5 minutes, until golden brown and crisp.

HAMBURGER CASSEROLE

Servings: 6 | Prep: 20m | Cooks: 20m | Total: 40m

NUTRITION FACTS

Calories: 457 | Carbohydrates: 56.1g | Fat: 15.3g | Protein: 24.7g | Cholesterol: 91mg

INGREDIENTS

- 1 pound ground beef
- 1 (14.5 ounce) can peeled and diced tomatoes
- 1 onion, chopped
- 1 (15 ounce) can whole kernel corn, drained
- 1 stalk celery, chopped
- 1/4 cup taco sauce
- 8 ounces egg noodles
- 1 (1 ounce) package taco seasoning mix
- 1 (15 ounce) can chili

DIRECTIONS

1. Preheat oven to 250 degrees F (120 degrees C).

2. In a large skillet over medium heat, combine the ground beef, onion and celery and saute for 10 minutes, or until the meat is browned and the onion is tender. Drain the fat and set aside.
3. In a separate saucepan, cook noodles according to package directions. When cooked, drain the water and stir in the meat mixture, chili, tomatoes, corn, taco sauce, and taco seasoning mix. Mix well and place entire mixture into a 10x15-inch baking dish.
4. Bake in the preheated oven until thoroughly heated and bubbling, about 20 minutes.

PORK CHALUPAS

Servings: 16 | Prep: 15m | Cooks: 9h | Total: 9h15m

NUTRITION FACTS

Calories: 474 | Carbohydrates: 57.8g | Fat: 14.9g | Protein: 26.4g | Cholesterol: 45mg

INGREDIENTS

- 1 (4 pound) pork shoulder roast
- 2 tablespoons salt
- 1 pound dried pinto beans
- 2 tablespoons dried oregano
- 3 (4 ounce) cans diced green chile peppers
- 2 tablespoons garlic powder
- 2 tablespoons chili powder
- 16 flour tortillas
- 2 tablespoons ground cumin

DIRECTIONS

1. Place the roast inside a slow cooker coated with cooking spray. In a separate bowl, stir together the beans, 2 cans of the chile peppers, chili powder, cumin, salt, oregano, and garlic powder. Pour the whole mixture over the roast, and add enough water so that the roast is mostly covered. Jiggle the roast a little to get some of the liquid underneath.
2. Cover, and cook on Low for 8 to 9 hours. Check after about 5 hours to make sure the beans have not absorbed all of the liquid. Add more water if necessary 1 cup at a time. Use just enough to keep the beans from drying out.
3. When the roast is fork-tender, remove it from the slow cooker, and place on a cutting board. Remove any bone and fat, then shred with forks. Return to the slow cooker, and stir in the remaining can of green chilies. Heat through, and serve with flour tortillas and your favorite toppings.

BEST BEEF ENCHILADAS

Servings: 8 | Prep: 25m | Cooks: 20m | Total: 45m

NUTRITION FACTS

Calories: 583 | Carbohydrates: 46.1g | Fat: 29.2g | Protein: 33g | Cholesterol: 94mg

INGREDIENTS

- 2 pounds ground beef
- 2 1/2 cups enchilada sauce
- 1/4 onion, finely chopped
- 1 1/2 teaspoons chili powder
- 1 cup shredded Cheddar cheese
- 1 clove garlic, minced
- 1/2 cup sour cream
- 1/2 teaspoon salt
- 1 tablespoon dried parsley
- 8 flour tortillas
- 1 tablespoon taco seasoning
- 1 (15 ounce) can black beans, rinsed and drained
- 1 teaspoon dried oregano
- 1 (4 ounce) can sliced black olives, drained
- 1/2 teaspoon ground black pepper
- 1/4 cup shredded Cheddar cheese

DIRECTIONS

1. Preheat oven to 350 degrees F (175 degrees C).
2. Cook and stir ground beef with onion in a skillet over medium heat until meat is crumbly and no longer pink, about 10 minutes. Drain grease. Stir 1 cup Cheddar cheese, sour cream, parsley, taco seasoning, oregano, and black pepper into the ground beef until cheese has melted. Mix in enchilada sauce, chili powder, garlic, and salt; bring to a simmer, reduce heat to low, and simmer until meat sauce is slightly thickened, about 5 minutes.
3. Lay a tortilla onto a work surface and spoon about 1/4 cup of meat sauce down the center of the tortilla. Top meat sauce with 1 tablespoon black beans and a sprinkling of black olives. Roll the tortilla up, enclosing the filling, and lay seam-side down into a 9x13-inch baking dish. Repeat with remaining tortillas. Spoon any remaining meat sauce over the enchiladas and scatter any remaining black beans and black olives over the top. Sprinkle tortillas with 1/4 cup Cheddar cheese.
4. Bake in the preheated oven until cheese topping is melted and enchiladas and sauce are bubbling, 20 to 22 minutes. Let stand 5 minutes before serving.

CHICKEN ENCHILADAS WITH CREAMY GREEN CHILE SAUCE

Servings: 6 | Prep: 30m | Cooks: 30m | Total: 1h

NUTRITION FACTS

Calories: 789 | Carbohydrates: 33.3g | Fat: 51.9g | Protein: 48.9g | Cholesterol: 172mg

INGREDIENTS

- 12 corn tortillas
- 2 cups chicken broth
- vegetable oil for pan-frying
- 1 cup sour cream
- 3 cooked boneless skinless chicken breast halves, shredded
- 1 (4 ounce) can chopped green chiles, drained
- 12 ounces shredded Monterey Jack cheese, divided
- 1/2 cup chopped green onions
- 3/4 cup minced onion
- 1/2 cup chopped fresh cilantro
- 1/4 cup butter
- 1/4 cup all-purpose flour

DIRECTIONS

1. Preheat oven to 375 degrees F (190 degrees C). Grease a 9x13-inch baking dish.
2. Heat 2 tablespoons of oil in a skillet over medium-high heat. Fry tortillas (1 at a time) for 5 seconds on each side to soften and make them pliable. Add more oil to pan as needed. Drain between layers of paper towel and keep warm.
3. Divide chicken, 10 ounces of Monterey Jack cheese, and onion among the 12 tortillas. Roll up each tortilla and place seam-side down in the prepared pan.
4. Melt butter in a saucepan over medium heat. Add flour and whisk until mixture begins to boil. Slowly add broth, stirring with a whisk until thickened. Mix in the sour cream and chiles, heating thoroughly but do not boil, stirring occasionally. Pour mixture over the enchiladas.
5. Bake in the preheated oven until bubbly and heated through, about 20 minutes. Top with remaining Monterey Jack cheese and bake for 5 more minutes. Garnish with chopped green onions and cilantro.

TRES LECHES CAKE

Servings: 8 | Prep: 25m | Cooks: 45m | Total: 2h30m | Additional: 1h20m

NUTRITION FACTS

Calories: 642 | Carbohydrates: 75g | Fat: 33g | Protein: 14.2g | Cholesterol: 241mg

INGREDIENTS

- 1 cup white sugar
- 1 1/2 teaspoons baking powder
- 5 egg yolks
- 1 (14 ounce) can sweetened condensed milk

- 5 egg whites
- 1 (12 fluid ounce) can evaporated milk
- 1/3 cup milk
- 1 pint heavy whipping cream
- 1 teaspoon vanilla extract
- 10 maraschino cherries
- 1 cup all-purpose flour

DIRECTIONS

1. Preheat oven to 350 degrees F (175 degrees C). Butter and flour bottom of a 9-inch springform pan.
2. Beat the egg yolks with 3/4 cup sugar until light in color and doubled in volume. Stir in milk, vanilla, flour and baking powder.
3. In a small bowl, beat egg whites until soft peaks form. Gradually add remaining 1/4 cup sugar. Beat until firm but not dry. Fold 1/3 of the egg whites into the yolk mixture to lighten it; fold in remaining egg whites. Pour batter into prepared pan.
4. Bake in preheated oven for 45 to 50 minutes or until cake tester inserted into the middle comes out clean. Allow to cool 10 minutes.
5. Loosen edge of cake with knife before removing side of pan. Cool cake completely on a wire rack.
6. Place cooled cake on a deep serving plate. Use a two-pronged meat fork or a cake tester to pierce the surface of cake.
7. Mix together condensed milk, evaporated milk and 1/4 cup of the whipping cream. Set aside 1 cup of the measured milk mixture and refrigerate for another use. Pour remaining milk mixture over cake slowly until absorbed. Whip the remaining whipping cream until it thickens and reaches spreading consistency. Frost cake with whipped cream and garnish with cherries. Store cake in the refrigerator.

MEXICAN CORN
Servings: 6 | Prep: 10m | Cooks: 10m | Total: 20m

NUTRITION FACTS

Calories: 359 | Carbohydrates: 38.2g | Fat: 22.7g | Protein: 8g | Cholesterol: 61mg

INGREDIENTS

- 2 (15.25 ounce) cans whole kernel corn, drained
- 10 jalapeno peppers, chopped
- 1 (8 ounce) package cream cheese
- 1 teaspoon garlic salt
- 1/4 cup butter

DIRECTIONS

1. In a medium saucepan combine corn, cream cheese, butter, jalapeno peppers and garlic salt. Cook over medium heat for about 10 minutes or until heated through, stirring constantly after cream cheese begins to melt.

MEXICAN WHOLE WHEAT FLOUR TORTILLAS
Servings: 18 | Prep: 15m | Cooks: 1m | Total: 1h36m

NUTRITION FACTS

Calories: 179 | Carbohydrates: 27.3g | Fat: 6.3g | Protein: 4.7g | Cholesterol: 0mg

INGREDIENTS

- 1 cup all-purpose flour
- 2 teaspoons salt
- 4 cups whole wheat bread flour
- 1 1/2 cups boiling water
- 1/2 cup shortening
- all-purpose flour for rolling

DIRECTIONS

1. In a large bowl, stir together 1 cup all-purpose flour, the whole wheat flour, and salt. Rub in the shortening by hand until the mixture is the texture of oatmeal. Make a well in the center, and pour in the boiling water. Mix with a fork until all of the water is evenly incorporated. Sprinkle with a bit of additional flour, and knead until the dough does not stick to your fingers. The dough should be smooth.
2. Make balls the size of golf balls, about 2 ounces each. Place them on a tray, and cover with a cloth. Let stand for at least 1 hour, or up to 8 hours.
3. Heat a griddle or large frying pan over high heat. On a lightly floured surface, roll out a tortilla to your preferred thinness. Fry one at a time. Place on the griddle for 10 seconds, as soon as you see a bubble on the top, flip the tortilla over. Let it cook for about 30 seconds, then flip and cook the other side for another 30 seconds. Roll out the next tortilla while you wait for that one to cook. Repeat until all of the balls have been cooked. Tortillas can be refrigerated or frozen.

MARGARITA GRILLED SHRIMP
Servings: 4 | Prep: 15m | Cooks: 5m | Total: 50m

NUTRITION FACTS

Calories: 188 | Carbohydrates: 1.3g | Fat: 11.1g | Protein: 18.7g | Cholesterol: 173mg

INGREDIENTS

- 1 pound shrimp, peeled and deveined

- 2 teaspoons tequila
- 3 tablespoons olive oil
- 1/4 teaspoon cayenne pepper
- 3 tablespoons chopped fresh cilantro
- 1/4 teaspoon salt
- 2 tablespoons fresh lime juice
- 4 bamboo skewers, soaked in water for 20 minutes
- 2 cloves garlic, minced

DIRECTIONS

1. Stir shrimp, olive oil, cilantro, lime juice, garlic, tequila, cayenne pepper, and salt together in a bowl. Cover the bowl with plastic wrap and refrigerate shrimp in marinade for 30 minutes.
2. Preheat an outdoor grill for high heat and lightly oil grate.
3. Remove shrimp from bowl and thread onto skewers; discard marinade.
4. Cook on the preheated grill until shrimp turn pink, 2 to 3 minutes per side.

CHIPOTLE SHRIMP TACOS

Servings: 6 | Prep: 15m | Cooks: 15m | Total: 30m

NUTRITION FACTS

Calories: 377 | Carbohydrates: 26.2g | Fat: 11.1 | Protein: 41.9g | Cholesterol: 316mg

INGREDIENTS

- 1 (12 ounce) package bacon, cut into small pieces
- 12 corn tortillas
- 1/2 onion, diced
- 1 cup chopped fresh cilantro
- 2 pounds large cooked shrimp - peeled, deveined, and cut in half
- 1 lime, juiced
- 3 chipotle peppers in adobo sauce, minced
- salt to taste (optional)

DIRECTIONS

1. In a large, deep skillet fry the bacon over medium-high heat until evenly brown. Drain the bacon fat. Add the onions to the pan with the bacon and cook 5 minutes or until the onions are translucent. Stir in the shrimp and chipotle chiles; cook 4 minutes or until heated through
2. Heat tortillas on an ungreased skillet over medium-high heat for 10 to 15 seconds. Turn and heat for another 5 to 10 seconds. Fill the heated tortillas with shrimp mixture. Sprinkle with cilantro, lime juice, and salt.

MEXICAN CORN ON THE COB (ELOTE)

Servings: 4 | Prep: 10m | Cooks: 10m | Total: 20m

NUTRITION FACTS

Calories: 386 | Carbohydrates: 28.9g | Fat: 29.1g | Protein: 8.4g | Cholesterol: 53mg

INGREDIENTS

- 4 ears corn, shucked
- 1/2 cup grated cotija cheese
- 1/4 cup melted butter
- 4 wedges lime (optional)
- 1/4 cup mayonnaise

DIRECTIONS

1. Preheat an outdoor grill for medium-high heat.
2. Grill corn until hot and lightly charred all over, 7 to 10 minutes, depending on the temperature of the grill. Roll the ears in melted butter, then spread evenly with mayonnaise. Sprinkle with cotija cheese and serve with a lime wedge.

SIMPLE SWEET AND SPICY CHICKEN WRAPS

Servings: 8 | Prep: 20m | Cooks: 15m | Total: 35m

NUTRITION FACTS

Calories: 488 | Carbohydrates: 44.7g | Fat: 22.6g | Protein: 26.6g | Cholesterol: 57mg

INGREDIENTS

- 1/2 cup mayonnaise
- 1 1/2 pounds skinless, boneless chicken breast halves - cut into thin strips
- 1/4 cup finely chopped seedless cucumber
- 1 cup thick and chunky salsa
- 1 tablespoon honey
- 1 tablespoon honey
- 1/2 teaspoon cayenne pepper
- 1/2 teaspoon cayenne pepper
- ground black pepper to taste
- 8 (10 inch) flour tortillas
- 2 tablespoons olive oil
- 1 (10 ounce) bag baby spinach leaves

DIRECTIONS

1. Mix together the mayonnaise, cucumber, 1 tablespoon of honey, 1/2 teaspoon of cayenne pepper, and black pepper in a bowl until smooth. Cover and refrigerate until needed.

2. Heat the olive oil in a skillet on medium-high heat, and cook and stir the chicken breast strips until they are beginning to turn golden and are no longer pink in the middle, about 8 minutes. Stir in the salsa, 1 tablespoon of honey, and 1/2 teaspoon of cayenne pepper. Reduce the heat to medium-low and simmer, stirring occasionally, until the flavors have blended, about 5 minutes.

3. Stack the tortillas, 4 at a time, in a microwave oven and heat until warm and pliable, 20 to 30 seconds per batch.

4. Spread each tortilla with 1 tablespoon of the mayonnaise-cucumber mixture, top with a layer of baby spinach leaves, and arrange about 1/2 cup of chicken mixture on the spinach leaves.

5. Fold the bottom of each tortilla up about 2 inches, and start rolling the burrito from the right side. When the burrito is half-rolled, fold the top of the tortilla down, enclosing the filling, and continue rolling to make a tight, compact cylinder.

EASY CHICKEN FAJITA SOUP

Servings: 10 | Prep: 20m | Cooks: 55m | Total: 1h15m

NUTRITION FACTS

Calories: 143 | Carbohydrates: 15.6g | Fat: 5.5g | Protein: 12.4g | Cholesterol: 24mg

INGREDIENTS

- 2 tablespoons vegetable oil
- 1 large onion, cut into thin strips
- 1 pound skinless, boneless chicken breasts, cut into strips
- 1 (14.5 ounce) can fire roasted diced tomatoes
- 1 (1.27 ounce) packet fajita seasoning
- 1 (15 ounce) can seasoned black beans
- 1 red bell pepper, cut into thin strips
- 1 (14 ounce) can chicken broth
- 1 green bell pepper, cut into thin strips
- 1 dash hot sauce
- 1 poblano pepper, cut into thin strips
- salt and pepper to taste

DIRECTIONS

1. Heat oil in a large soup pot over medium heat. Place chicken in the hot oil; cook, stirring only occasionally, until brown, about 10 minutes. Sprinkle fajita seasoning over the browned chicken and stir well to coat. Add the red and green bell pepper, poblano pepper, and onion to the seasoned chicken. Stir and cook over medium heat until the vegetables are soft, about 10 minutes.

106

2. Pour the fire roasted tomatoes, black beans, and chicken broth into the pot with the chicken and vegetables. Bring the soup to a boil over high heat, then reduce the heat to medium-low, and simmer uncovered for 30 minutes, stirring occasionally.
3. Season the soup with hot sauce, salt, and pepper to taste before serving.

TACO BAKE

Servings: 8 | Prep: 15m | Cooks: 25m | Total: 40m

NUTRITION FACTS

Calories: 413 | Carbohydrates: 15.4g | Fat: 26.9g | Protein: 25.9g | Cholesterol: 93mg

INGREDIENTS

- 1 1/2 pounds lean ground beef
- 1 (16 ounce) jar salsa
- 1 (1.25 ounce) package taco seasoning mix
- 2 cups shredded Monterey Jack cheese
- 1 (16 ounce) can refried beans

DIRECTIONS

1. Preheat oven to 325 degrees F (160 degrees C).
2. In a large, heavy skillet over medium-high heat, brown ground beef, and drain fat. Mix in dry taco seasoning.
3. Spoon browned meat into a 9x13 inch glass baking dish. Spoon a layer of refried beans over meat, then salsa. Top with shredded cheese.
4. Bake about 20 to 25 minutes in the preheated oven.

TEXAS CHICKEN QUESADILLAS

Servings: 8 | Prep: 20m | Cooks: 15m | Total: 35m

NUTRITION FACTS

Calories: 411 | Carbohydrates: 46.2g | Fat: 14.3g | Protein: 23.2g | Cholesterol: 48mg

INGREDIENTS

- 2 tablespoons vegetable oil, divided
- 1/2 cup barbeque sauce
- 1 onion, sliced into rings
- 1/2 cup shredded sharp Cheddar cheese
- 1 tablespoon honey
- 1/2 cup shredded Monterey Jack cheese

- 2 skinless, boneless chicken breast halves - cut into strips
- 8 (10 inch) flour tortillas

DIRECTIONS

1. Preheat oven to 350 degrees F (175 degrees C).
2. In a large, deep skillet, heat 1 tablespoon oil over medium high heat. Slowly cook and stir onion until translucent. Mix in honey. Stir until onion is golden brown, about 5 minutes. Remove from skillet and set aside.
3. Place remaining oil and chicken in the skillet over medium high heat. Cook until chicken is no longer pink. Stir in barbeque sauce and evenly coat chicken.
4. Layer 4 tortillas individually with chicken, onions, Cheddar cheese and Monterey Jack cheese. Top with remaining tortillas.
5. One or two at a time, place layered tortillas on a large baking sheet. Bake uncovered in the preheated oven 20 minutes, or until cheese is melted. Do not let tortillas become too crisp. Remove from heat. Cut into quarters to serve.

MEXICAN QUESADILLA CASSEROLE
Servings: 8 | Prep: 15m | Cooks: 25m | Total: 45m

NUTRITION FACTS

Calories: 493 | Carbohydrates: 50.1g | Fat: 21.2g | Protein: 26.6 g | Cholesterol: 65mg

INGREDIENTS

- cooking spray
- 2 teaspoons chili powder
- 1 pound ground beef
- 1 teaspoon ground cumin
- 1/2 cup chopped onion
- 1 teaspoon minced garlic
- 1 (15 ounce) can tomato sauce
- 1/2 teaspoon dried oregano
- 1 (15 ounce) can black beans, rinsed and drained
- 1/2 teaspoon red pepper flakes
- 1 (14.5 ounce) can diced tomatoes with lime juice and cilantro (such as RO*TEL)
- 6 flour tortillas
- 1 (8.75 ounce) can whole kernel sweet corn, drained
- 2 cups shredded Cheddar cheese
- 1 (4.5 ounce) can chopped green chiles, drained

DIRECTIONS

1. Preheat oven to 350 degrees F (175 degrees C). Prepare a 13x9-inch baking dish with cooking spray.
2. Heat a large skillet over medium-high heat. Cook and stir beef and onion in the hot skillet until beef is completely browned, 5 to 7 minutes; drain and discard grease.
3. Stir tomato sauce, black beans, diced tomatoes with lime juice and cilantro, corn, and chopped green chiles into the ground beef mixture; season with chili powder, cumin, garlic, oregano, and red pepper flakes. Reduce heat to low and cook mixture at a simmer for 5 minutes.
4. Spread about 1/2 cup beef mixture into the bottom of the prepared baking dish; top with 3 tortillas, overlapping as needed. Spread another 1/2 cup beef mixture over the tortillas. Sprinkle 1 cup Cheddar cheese over beef. Finish with layers of remaining tortillas, beef mixture, and Cheddar cheese, respectively.
5. Bake in preheated oven until heated throughout and the cheese is melted, about 15 minutes. Cool 5 minutes before serving.

POLVORONES DE CANELE (CINNAMON COOKIES)
Servings: 24 | Prep: 20m | Cooks: 20m | Total: 1h | Additional: 20m

NUTRITION FACTS

Calories: 126 | Carbohydrates:13.6 g | Fat: 7.8g | Protein: 0.9g | Cholesterol: 20mg

INGREDIENTS

- 1 cup butter
- 1 teaspoon vanilla extract
- 1/2 cup confectioners' sugar
- 1 1/2 cups all-purpose flour
- 1/2 teaspoon ground cinnamon
- 1 cup confectioners' sugar
- 1/4 teaspoon salt
- 1 teaspoon ground cinnamon

DIRECTIONS

1. Preheat oven to 350 degrees F (175 degrees C). Grease cookie sheets.
2. In a medium bowl, cream together 1/2 cup confectioners' sugar and butter until smooth. Stir in vanilla. Combine flour, salt, and 1/2 teaspoon of cinnamon; stir into the creamed mixture to form a stiff dough. Shape dough into 1 inch balls. Mix together 1 cup confectioners' sugar and 1 teaspoon cinnamon; roll balls in cinnamon mixture.
3. Bake for 15 to 20 minutes in preheated oven, or until nicely browned. Cool cookies on wire racks.

SWEET CORN TOMALITO

Servings: 8 | Prep: 20m | Cooks: 1h | Total: 1h20m

NUTRITION FACTS

Calories: 174 | Carbohydrates: 26.7g | Fat: 7.3g | Protein: 2.4g | Cholesterol: 1mg

INGREDIENTS

- 5 tablespoons margarine, softened
- 1/2 cup cornmeal
- 1/4 cup masa harina
- 1 teaspoon baking powder
- 1/3 cup white sugar
- 1/2 teaspoon salt
- 1/2 cup water
- 4 teaspoons milk
- 2 cups frozen whole-kernel corn, thawed

DIRECTIONS

1. In a medium bowl, mix together the margarine, masa flour, and sugar until light and fluffy. In a food processor or blender, blend one cup of the corn kernels with the water and cornmeal just until smooth. Stir into the masa mixture. Mix in the remaining corn, baking powder, salt, and milk until the batter is smooth. Pour into a double boiler.
2. Place the tomalito over a large saucepan of simmering water, and cover tightly with aluminum foil. Steam for 50 to 60 minutes, or until firm. Check water occasionally, and refill if necessary. Stir pudding before serving to give it a consistent texture. Serve in small scoops.

MEXICAN SOUR CREAM RICE

Servings: 6 | Prep: 20m | Cooks: 30m | Total: 50m

NUTRITION FACTS

Calories: 287 | Carbohydrates: 36.9g | Fat: 11.4g | Protein: 9.9g | Cholesterol: 34mg

INGREDIENTS

- 1 cup uncooked long grain white rice
- 1 cup shredded Monterey Jack cheese, divided
- 1 (14 ounce) can chicken broth
- 1 (8.75 ounce) can whole kernel corn, drained
- 1 cup reduced fat sour cream
- 1/4 cup finely chopped fresh cilantro

- 1 (4 ounce) can diced green chile peppers
- salt and ground black pepper to taste

DIRECTIONS

1. In a large pot, bring the rice and chicken broth to a boil. Reduce heat to low, cover, and simmer 20 minutes.
2. Preheat oven to 350 degrees F (175 degrees C). Lightly grease a 1-1/2 quart casserole dish.
3. In the pot with the cooked rice, mix the sour cream, green chile peppers, 1/2 cup Monterey Jack cheese, corn, and cilantro. Season with salt and pepper. Transfer to the prepared casserole dish, and top with remaining cheese.
4. Bake uncovered 30 minutes in the preheated oven, until cheese is bubbly and lightly browned.

AVOCADO SALAD

Servings: 6 | Prep: 10m | Cooks: 0m | Total: 10m

NUTRITION FACTS

Calories: 126 | Carbohydrates: 10.2g | Fat: 10g | Protein: 2.1g | Cholesterol: 0mg

INGREDIENTS

- 2 avocados - peeled, pitted and diced
- 1/4 cup chopped fresh cilantro
- 1 sweet onion, chopped
- 1/2 lime, juiced
- 1 green bell pepper, chopped
- salt and pepper to taste
- 1 large ripe tomato, chopped

DIRECTIONS

1. In a medium bowl, combine avocados, onion, bell pepper, tomato, cilantro and lime juice. Gently toss until evenly coated. Season with salt and pepper.

Made in the USA
Monee, IL
02 October 2022